Walter J Malden

Rational pig keeping to ensure profit

Walter J Malden

Rational pig keeping to ensure profit

ISBN/EAN: 9783742836717

Manufactured in Europe, USA, Canada, Australia, Japa

Cover: Foto ©knipser5 / pixelio.de

Manufactured and distributed by brebook publishing software
(www.brebook.com)

Walter J Malden

Rational pig keeping to ensure profit

Farm Field & Fireside

SERIES.—No. I.

RATIONAL PIG KEEPING

TO ENSURE PROFIT.

BY

W. J. MALDEN.

*Late Superintendent of Royal Agricultural Society's Experimental Farms, Woburn
Professor of Agriculture, Downton College; Agricultural Superintendent
Royal Dublin Society, &c., &c., &c.*

ILLUSTRATED.

IN TEN SECTIONS.

I. PRINCIPAL BREEDS.

II. SELECTION OF STOCK.

III. HOUSING.

IV. FOODS.

V. BREEDING.

VI. MANAGEMENT.

VII. THE COTTAGER'S PIG.

VIII. AILMENTS.

IX. THE PIG TRADE.

X. PIG CALENDAR.

EACH WITH MANY SUB-SECTIONS.

LONDON:

WILLIAM A. MAY,

"FARM, FIELD AND FIRESIDE" OFFICE,

1, Essex Street, Strand, W.C.

PREFACE.

THE large number of questions relating to Pig Keeping which are asked in the inquiry columns of agricultural newspapers indicate that there are many pig keepers and would-be pig keepers who require an inexpensive but comprehensive book as a guide in purchasing and managing their pigs. This book contains all that is best in the writer's experience of their management, which dates from earliest boyhood, and an endeavour has been made to place it before the reader in simple language, and in such a form that he may obtain information on any point with little trouble.

The illustrations of breeds are specially prepared, as are some of the designs for housing. Thanks, however, are due to Messrs. Richmond & Chandler, Barford & Perkins, and Hill & Smith, for illustrations they have kindly supplied.

W. J. MALDEN.

CARDINGTON,
  NEAR BEDFORD.

RATIONAL PIG KEEPING.

SECTION I.

BREEDS.

WILD BREEDS.

THE pig, or hog, is the descendant of the wild hog, *Sus aper*, which is indigenous to Europe, Asia, and Northern Africa. Representatives of the hog family not descended from the wild hog are found in the Eastern Archipelago, South Africa, America, and other places; but these are not of practical interest to the farmer, as they have not found a place in domestication. In America the peccary was the only representative of the swine family until European pigs were imported. The enormous number of pigs found there now in a state of domestication are all descendants of the wild hog of the Old World. In Australia, South Africa, and practically all places where white men make their home, the pig is an important source of food. From the most remote ages it has supplied man with food, and the fact that it was considered unclean under the Levitical and Mahomedan laws did not prevent its popularity being maintained throughout the rest of the world.

At the present time, although breeds of cattle and sheep have been greatly improved, it is a highly important section of the meat-producing animals.

The Wild Hog.

The wild hog varies very much in appearance, in accordance with its age and the climate in which it is reared. The colour in the more temperate latitudes is a dusky brown, with black spots and streaks. The skin is very thick, and covered with coarse bristles intermixed with soft wool. As compared with the domesticated pig he is lean and gaunt, given to roving, and able to travel at great speed; in fact he is better suited for fast travelling than for the laying-on of meat. Being both strong and ferocious, he does not appear likely to thrive in confinement; but, surprising as it may seem, his offspring are soon domesticated, and rapidly develop flesh-making propensities. On the other hand, if domesticated pigs are turned adrift they soon regain their old characteristics, and rapidly degenerate. Of all domesticated animals they are the most quickly improved by favourable conditions of diet and confinement, but they are equally susceptible to unfavourable influences. For this reason the pig keeper finds it necessary to exercise care in their management, and in the proper selection of mates, so that a high standard (once obtained) may be maintained. The typical features of the wild hog are a light fore-quarter, long head, long, narrow frame on long legs, coarse skin, and a generally gaunt and unthriving appearance. Domestication and an ample supply of suitable food, together with judicious mating and selection, rapidly change the animal— the most noticeable features being the enlargement of various parts of the body. The stomach and intestines increase, the sides deepen, the back lengthens, and the limbs are set wider, thus developing the valuable portions; while, simultaneously, the bone becomes finer, the skin thinner, and the proportion of waste to profitable meat decreases. The food consumed by such an animal is thus devoted to the production of meat rather than offal. A comparison between a modern highly-bred animal and a wild pig reveals one of the most striking instances of the skill of the stock-keeper.

The Domestic Pig.

As in the case of all domesticated animals where trouble has been taken to improve them, the more valuable features are most permanently retained where care has been bestowed for the longest time: the characteristics of pedigree are thus obtained. The value of pedigree is chiefly that valuable features have been produced and maintained uninterruptedly for a number of generations, and that these features are most difficult to eradicate, a fixity of type having been obtained; also that these features will be transmitted to offspring. The longer a breed has been kept under beneficial circumstances the more valuable is it found in improving inferior breeds with which

it is crossed. The native breeds of England were
not subjected to much improvement at the hands of
breeders until within the last century. It was difficult to convey pigs from one part of the country to
another; and improvements made in the breeding
were more often due to selection than to the intro-
duction of fresh strains of improved breeds. Still
before railways were introduced importations of
foreign animals had been made, notably those from
China and Naples. The Chinese pig — found in
China, Siam, Malacca, the Burmahs, and other
Eastern countries—has been under the influence of
domestication for a long period, and has apparently
been well cared for and well managed, as it has
become a marvellously quick feeder, its well-shaped
body being typical of meat-producing. There are
several types of Chinese pigs, but all fatten readily.
They are small, and the flesh is of fine texture,
rendering them highly suitable for mating with
coarser breeds. In addition to this, and notwithstanding their fattening properties, they are very
prolific. The Neapolitan is a black breed, less prolific
than the Chinese. It is short on the legs, long in
the body, somewhat deficient in hair, short in the
face, and possesses small erect ears. To these two
breeds English pig keepers are greatly indebted.
The native breeds of England before their introduc-
tion were coarse unthrifty animals, better suited to
find a living in forests and wastes than to turn to
profitable account farm-grown produce. Under the
influence of these breeds, together with skill on the
part of the breeders, the country now possesses

several breeds of great excellence, and really coarse pigs are rare.

ORIGINAL ENGLISH BREEDS.

The original breeds of the country were very numerous, but were comprised in two classes. The Small, having upright ears, skin generally dark in colour, and resembling in many characteristics the wild boar, were found in Scotland, the North of England, and hilly districts, where little pains were taken to domesticate them. The Large, having long bodies, long ears, skin generally white or spotted, were met with in Southern and Midland counties, where more trouble had been taken to develop their better points. The development of existing breeds has been chiefly effected during the present century, and no small portion of the improvement has been made during the last half of the century. Local breeds have practically disappeared, though there are many men now living who can remember them. Still more can remember the lean, thriftless animals, by no means rare, within the past half century. The influence of improved breeds has been felt in all districts, and now they are rarely seen. In some outlying parts of Ireland they are occasionally met with, but even there they are fast disappearing. The features of the original breeds of pigs found in different parts of the country were briefly as follows:— Yorkshire, very large, heavy feeders, difficult to fatten, colour dirty-white or yellow, with black spots, legs long, sides flat, backs narrow, loins weak, ears long, hair short and wiry, bones and offal large. Lincolnshire, white, with long straight bodies, round carcases, fine skin and hair, well formed heads with erect ears pointing somewhat forward, and with tips slightly curved: one of the best breeds. Leicestershire, the typical pig of the Midlands, large, ungainly, flat-sided animals, light in colour, with spots of brown or black. A well-shaped head was its chief merit. Suffolk, white, long-legged, long-bodied, narrow-backed, broad forehead, short hair with many bristles : a difficult pig to feed. Norfolk, practically the same as the Lincolnshire. Northamptonshire, large-bodied, large-boned, bristly animals, covered with coarse, white hair, legs short, and ears so long that sometimes they trailed upon the ground. They fed to a great size, but were expensive to fatten. The Shropshire were very similar. Cheshire, the pigs when fully grown stood from $3\frac{1}{2}$ to $4\frac{1}{2}$ feet high, their colour black and white, white, and blue and white, bodies long, backs narrow, sides flat, bones large, and limbs long, heads long, and ears so large and drooping as to almost prevent the animals seeing, the skin loose and coarse. Notwithstanding their coarseness they were fairly good feeders. Gloucestershire, large, gaunt, and coarse, long-legged, and profitless. Herefordshire, very similar to Northamptonshire, but rather smaller, the quality being superior, excellently suited for bacon. Wiltshire, coarse and large, light-coloured. Cornwall, a large white breed, extremely narrow, and generally unprofitable. Berkshire, large, sandy, or whitish brown, spotted regularly with dark brown spots, hair long and thin, somewhat curly, but no bristles, ears erect; ranked very high among original breeds on account of its fine flesh and aptitude to fatten. Hampshire, two breeds, differing chiefly in size; colour white, or black and white. The small was a thrifty animal. Sussex, a large breed called the Rudgwick, was one of the largest in England. There appears to be a doubt as to whether the coloured pig was descended from the spotted Berkshire or the black and white Essex. They were of medium size, of good quality generally, but of somewhat heavy bone.

From the above remarks it will be seen that the pigs found in various parts of the country have greatly altered. Little trace of original features can be found now in many districts, most of the animals being closely related to one of the few important modern breeds.

Modern Breeds.

Although some of the continental breeds possess valuable features, very few of them are imported to improve English breeds. This is due to the fact that English breeds have been raised to such a high state of perfection that new blood is not required to improve them. Judicious mating with home breeds is sufficient to maintain the standard they have reached. The excellence of British breeds is well illustrated by the fact that they are more highly appreciated in countries, such as America, Australia, and Southern Africa, which possess no native breeds, than are breeds from other countries. In some parts of America the Poland China is in high favour, and other crosses have their place, but by far the greater number of pigs in those countries have an English origin. It is greatly to the credit of English breeders that this should be the case; as they had no better conditions to start on, the result has been largely due to judicious selection and management.

The modern British breeds are now comprised in the Large, Middle, and Small Yorkshires, the Berkshire, the Tamworth, the Essex, or the Suffolk, and the Dorset, the latter being comprised in the Small Black breed. A few offshoots of these breeds possess local names, such as the Bedfordshire, which, as now found, is little other than a cross of the Large and Middle Whites; but they are not distinct breeds. The Chester White is an American breed which took its name from Chester county, Pennsylvania, and not from the English city. They are believed to be descended from some large white pigs imported from Bedfordshire at the beginning of the century. The three Yorkshire breeds, commonly spoken of as the Large, Middle, and Small Whites, cover a wide range—in fact, supply anything from the largest bacon pig to the plumpest little roaster, at the same time they illustrate the effect that public opinion has had on those who have taken upon themselves to improve the White breeds. The native pig was too coarse, and too slow in coming to maturity, and these were the first points to be rectified. Well-grown native Yorkshire pigs frequently weighed a thousand pounds, and occasionally some hundreds of pounds in addition; but this weight was only obtained after the consumption of so much food as to leave but little profit, while the meat thus made was coarse and not too finely flavoured.

THE LARGE WHITE BREED.

A large number of breeds were at one time or another crossed with the Yorkshire pig, and as these included the China and the Neapolitan the coarseness gradually disappeared, but it was not until 1851 that it acquired a reputation for rapid maturity. Joseph Tuley, of Keighley, wrought great improvements in the breed, and to him is due the credit of laying the foundation to the modern Large White breed. From the time Tuley exhibited his animals at the Royal Agricultural Show at Windsor, in 1851, the breed obtained prominence, and at the hands of many skilled breedmakers it has become one of the best, if not quite the best, in the world. While producing only a reasonable amount of offal, and meat of good quality, it is capable of growing to a weight of thirty stone in twelve months. The Large White is hardy and prolific; the young are sturdy, and not very liable to rheumatism and cramp. It is, in fact, a pig easy to raise. The Large White has very much improved in quality during recent years, as breeders have directed their attention to this matter. The taste for meat of fine quality has greatly increased, and the value of an animal is not altogether gauged by its size, but rather by the readiness with which it can be sold. This has had a tendency—and very properly so— to cause breeders of the Large Whites to sacrifice some little of the size for quality, and the quality of a well-bred Large White is now very similar to that of a Middle White. The following is the standard of excellence adopted by the National Pig Breeders' Association in relation to the Large White breed:—

Colour.—White, free from black hairs, and, as far as possible, blue spots on the skin.

Head.—Moderately long, face slightly dished, snout broad, not too much turned up, jowl not too heavy, wide between ears.

Ears.—Long, thin, slightly inclined forward and fringed with fine hair.

Neck.—Long, and proportionately full to the shoulders.

Chest.—Wide and deep.

Shoulders.—Level across the top, not too wide, free from coarseness.

Legs.—Straight and well set, level with the outside of the body, with flat bone.

Pasterns.—Short and springy.

Feet.—Strong, even, and wide.

Back.—Long, level, and wide from neck to rump.

Loin.—Broad.

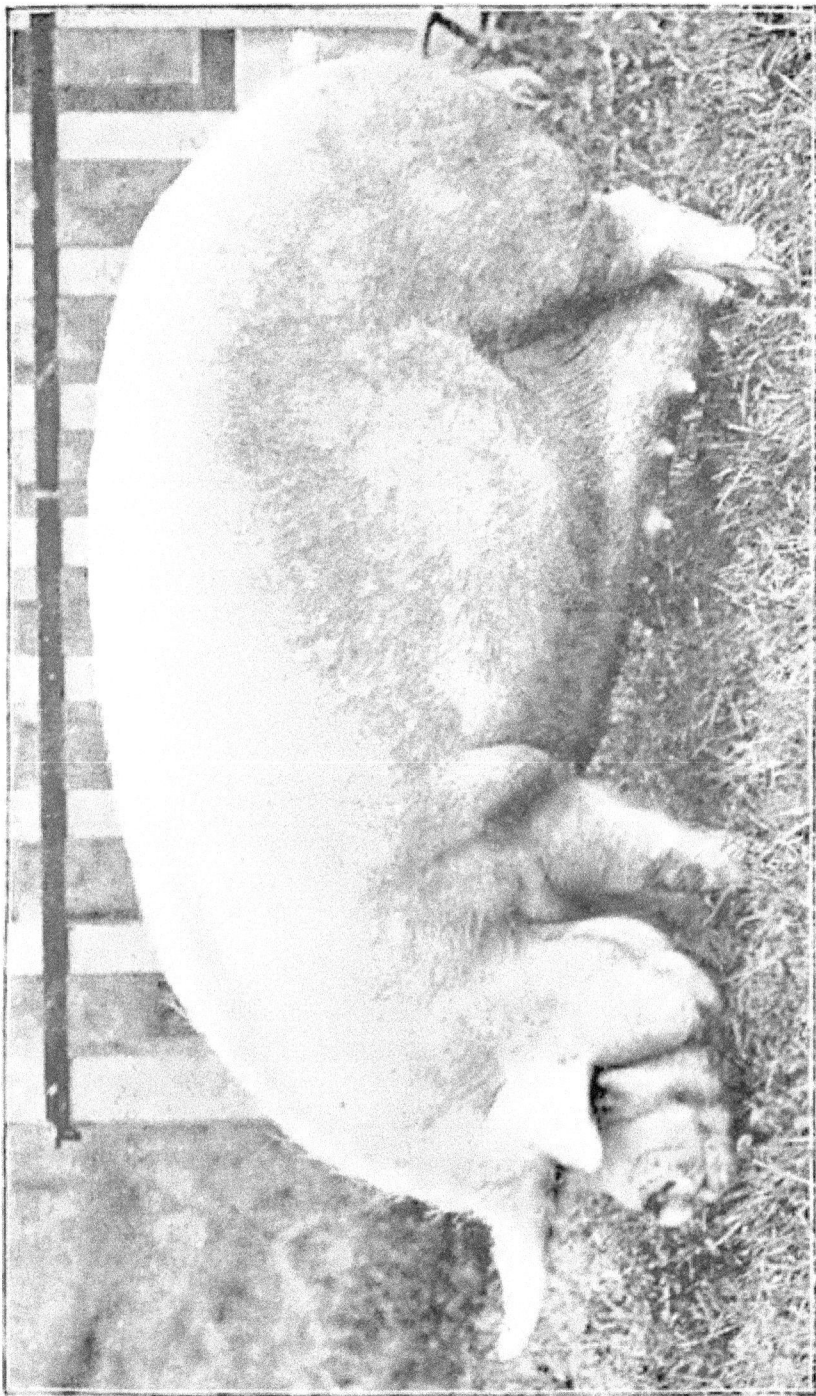

Fig. 1.—Mr. Edwin Buss' Large White Sow_ "Elphicks Daisy 2nd."

Tail.—Set high, stout and long, but not coarse, with tassel of fine hair.

Sides.—Deep.

Ribs.—Well sprung.

Belly.—Full, but not flabby, and straight underline.

Flank.—Thick and well let down.

Quarters.—Long and wide.

Hams.—Broad, full and deep to hocks.

Coat.—Long and moderately fine.

Action.—Firm and free.

Skin.—Not too thick ; quite free from wrinkles.

Large bred pigs do not develop their points fully till some months old, the pig at five months often proving at a year or fifteen months old a much better animal than could be anticipated at the earlier age. Size and quality are a most important point.

Objections.—Black hairs, black spots, a curly coat, a coarse mane, short snout, inbent knees, hollowness at back of shoulders.

With a standard so carefully drawn up, breeders should not go far wrong. The points are well recognised by breeders as being essential to the welfare of the breeder, and there is little fear that the breed will be tampered with. The large exportation of these pigs indicates how well they are appreciated abroad, where often they have to exist under less favourable conditions than at home, as it is a breed which is frequently called upon to travel to some extent in search of food. While in a store condition it is highly important that the feature of inbent legs is guarded against ; it is equally important that the legs are well placed when the animal is being fattened, as the heavy carcass requires strong supports.

THE SMALL WHITE BREED.

The call for small joints and meat of fine quality set breeders the task of making a breed in which quality both in outward appearance and in firmness of the texture of meat, together with an early maturity, should be the main features. The outcome of this was the Small White breed. This breed illustrates what may be done when skill and care are bestowed on a breed of animals, for it is one of the greatest triumphs of the breedmaker. It is not necessarily the best pig, but it would be difficult to imagine an animal which combines to a higher degree quality, early maturity, fine-grained flesh, minimum of offal, and shapeliness. The meat is inclined to be too fat, and the constitution has undoubtedly suffered somewhat in the fining, therefore when quite pure bred they are not best adapted to the purposes of the farmer. However, the breed has its place, for when crossed with coarser animals possessing vigorous constitutions, the offspring are improved. The young pigs of this breed are not very robust, and are liable to rheumatism and cramp, unless very warmly housed. Nor can they assimilate a large quantity of very rich food without danger of apoplexy. In the straw yards they are liable to be injured by cattle.

Those who desire to breed animals to produce small hams and small joints of pork free from coarseness cannot find a more suitable animal; however, if allowed to become very fat, they are wasteful in cooking. The following is the standard of excellence adopted by the National Pig Breeders' Association in relation to the Small White breed :—

Colour.—Pure white.

Head.—Very short and dished, snout broad and turned up, jowl very full, broad between the ears.

Ears.—Small, short, and erect.

Neck.—Short and thick.

Chest.—Full and broad.

Shoulders.—Full and wide.

Legs.—Short, set well outside the body, fine bone.

Pasterns.—Short and springy.

Feet.—Small.

Back.—Broad, level, and straight.

Loin.—Wide.

Tail.—High set, small and fine, with tassel of fine hair.

Girth.—As deep as possible consistent with length.

Sides.—Deep.

Ribs.—Well sprung.

Belly.—Deep and near ground.

Flank. —Thick and well let down.

Quarters.—Wide and full.

Hams.—Deep, wide, full, and well rounded.

Coat.—Fine and silky.

Action.—Free and firm.

Skin.—Fine, quite free from wrinkles.

The general appearance of animals, small, thick and compact when compared with other breeds.

Objections.—Black hairs, black or blue spots, coarse hair, inbent knees, hollowness at back of shoulder, wrinkled skin.

THE MIDDLE WHITE BREED.

Between the Large White and the Small White breeds there was a wide gap. By some the Large White was considered too big, and by others the Small White were thought to lack size. It was therefore not surprising that those who saw the good points of the two breeds should conceive the idea of making a breed which should as far as possible combine all that was best in them. The breeds representing size and quality were therefore crossed, and the Middle White was the result. In size it more nearly approaches the Large White than the Small White. The diminutive nose of the Small breed gives place to a stronger and more characteristic snout, and altogether the animal is suggestive of robustness without coarseness. The Large White has been toned down so that there is not a great deal of difference between them now, and had the breed been in the condition it is at present there would have been less room for the Middle White. The Middle White is a good farmer's pig, being suitable for slaughtering at almost any age. Its robustness fits it for the yards or for grazing. It is also a good breed for crossing with less well-bred

Fig. 2.—Mr. Sanders Spencer's Middle White Sow "Holywell Middlesborough."

animals, as it fines down those which are coarse, and increases those which are diminutive or too finely bred.

The following is the standard of excellence adopted by the National Pig Breeders' Association in relation to the Middle White breed :—

Colour.—White, free from black hairs and blue spots on the skin.

Head.—Moderately short, face dished, snout broad and turned up, jowl full, wide between the ears.

Ears.—Fairly large, carried erect and fringed with fine hair.

Neck.—Medium length, proportionately full to the shoulders.

Chest.—Wide and deep.

Shoulders.—Level across the top, moderately wide, free from coarseness.

Leg.—Straight and well set, level without-side of the body with fine bone.

Pasterns.—Short and springy.

Feet.—Strong, even, and wide.

Back.—Long, level, and wide from rump.

Loin.—Broad.

Tail.—Set high, moderate length, but not coarse, with tassel of fine hair.

Sides.—Deep.

Ribs.—Well sprung.

Belly.—Full, but not flabby and straight underline.

Flank.—Thick, and well let down.

Quarters.—Long and wide.

Hams.—Broad, full and deep to hocks.

Coat.—Long, fine, and silky.

Action.—Firm and free.

Skin.—Fine and quite free from wrinkles.

Objections.—Black hairs, black or blue spots, a coarse mane, inbent knees, hollowness at back of shoulders, wrinkled skin.

THE BERKSHIRE.

The Berkshire is the most important of the coloured breeds. It has now been bred to a whole black colour except the feet and a small blaze on the face, which are white. The broken colour of half a century ago is not permitted. The small quantity of white is evidently adhered to with the view of preventing too much breeding with the smaller black breeds, which possess exceptionally fine quality, but a tendency to produce a large proportion of fat. In point of usefulness the Berkshire is very similar to the Middle White, being suitable to pig keepers of all classes. It attains a large size when fully matured, but may be said to be in a state of maturity all its life, as it is fit to kill at any age. It makes a good roaster, an excellent porker at eight or ten stones, a good general purpose pig from ten to fifteen stones, or may be turned to bacon anywhere from that to forty stones, as may be desired. It is prolific and hardy, thriving on food of almost any kind. The Berkshire Society have issued to the leading Agricultural Show Societies the following instructions as guides to judges in making their awards :—

"We recommend that a perfectly black face, or a black foot or black tail, should disqualify a' pig in the

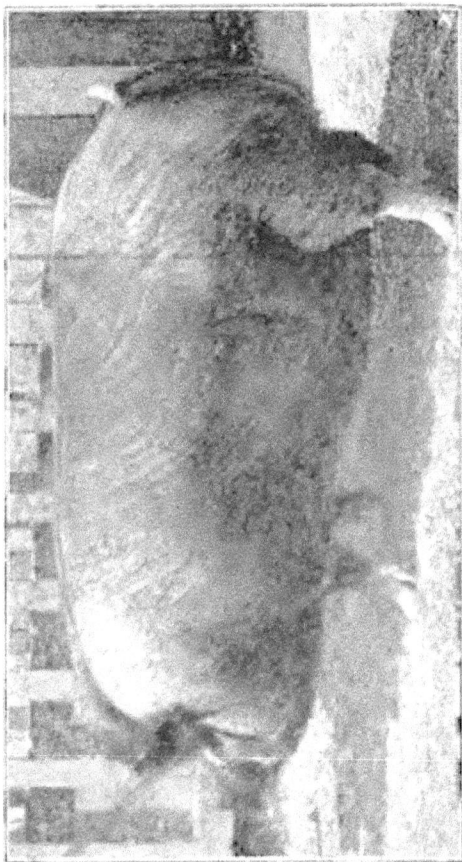

Fig. 3.—Mr. Edwin Buss' Berkshire Sow " Elphicks Matchless."

show yard. White or sandy spots on the top or sides of the animal, or a decidedly white ear should be a disqualification. Any description of colouring, staining or clipping should also be a disqualification. White on the ear or under the throat, or on the underlines of the body, should be considered objectionable. A rose back should be an objection. Either too much or too little white in the place of the proper recognised markings should be an objection, also to be noted in the competition."

The Berkshire is found in all districts, and has achieved an enviable notoriety in America. It is almost a model breed, and it appears difficult to suggest alteration without running the risk of doing injury in some other direction. It is most important to keep a good coating of hair on, as this not only indicates vigour, but trueness of breeding. The temptation to acquire the appearance of fineness of quality, combined with early maturity, is very difficult for some to resist, as by crossing with the smaller breeds they are easily obtained. No pig shows itself to greater advantage in the show-yard, as when well haired the glossy coat acts as a fine set-off to the shapely outline. It is essentially a farmer's pig, and it is most desirable that the type should be maintained without allowing its vigour to be impaired.

THE TAMWORTH BREED.

The Tamworth is a breed which did not achieve a very widespread popularity until recent years, although it is stated it was occasionally used to cross

with the Berkshire early in the century. As a breed
it has without doubt been much improved of late.
Owing to the influence of some of its admirers it has
been brought into public notice, and they have
received support from some of the large bacon
curers, who are favourably impressed with it on
account of the high quality of the meat for bacon
purposes. The development of more rapid maturity
in other breeds has doubtless been done at the
expense of the lean meat; consequently, where care
is not exercised the bacon from them is too fat for
the popular taste. The improvement in the
Tamworth is largely due to selection, though no
doubt other breeds have been called in to help. The
Tamworth is comparatively slow in attaining
maturity, but when mature the lean meat is fine and
delicately flavoured, and the fat is fine and not gross
in texture or taste. Its chief value is as a bacon pig,
and as it is slow in coming to maturity it is not
found so profitable as the quicker maturing breeds
for general purposes. Its red skin distinguishes it
from other British breeds. It makes an excellent
cross with other breeds which have too great tendency
to produce fat. The following is the standard of
excellence adopted by the National Pig Breeders'
Association in relation to the Tamworth breed:—

Colour.—Golden-red hair on a flesh-coloured skin
free from black.

Head.—Fairly long, snout moderately long, and
quite straight, face slightly dished, wide between ears.

Ears.—Rather large with fine fringe, carried rigid,
but inclined slightly forward.

Fig. 4.—Mr. R. Ibbotson's Tamworth Sow "Knowle Rosy" 5592.

Neck.—Fairly long and muscular, especially in boar.

Chest.—Wide and deep.

Shoulders.—Fine standing and well set.

Legs.—Strong and shapely with plenty of bone, and set well outside body.

Pasterns.—Strong and sloping.

Feet.—Strong and of fair size.

Back.—Long and straight.

Loin.—Strong and broad.

Tail.—Set on high and well tasselled.

Girth.—Deep and full round heart.

Sides.—Long and deep.

Ribs.—Well sprung, and extending well up to flank.

Belly.—Deep, with straight under line.

Flank.—Full and well let down.

Quarters.—Long, wide, and straight from hip to tail.

Hams.—Broad and full, and well let down to hock.

Coat.—Abundant, long, straight, and fine.

Action.—Firm and free.

Objections.—Black hairs, very light or ginger hair, curly coat, coarse mane, black spots on skin, slouch or drooping ears, short or turned-up snout, heavy shoulders, wrinkled skin, inbent knees, hollowness at back of shoulders.

SMALL BLACK BREEDS.

The Essex breed has become a black one chiefly owing to crossing with the Neapolitan. The breed as now found is small, but of fine quality, resembling the Small White in that it comes to maturity very quickly, and lays on rather too much fat in proportion to lean. It also makes good pork at any age. The offal is small, and altogether the animal turns to good account the food which it consumes.

The Suffolks, which differ only in a small degree from the Essex, are generally supposed to have been raised from the Essex crossed with other breeds, and they are usually classed together. The Dorset has many points in common with the Essex, but its skin is of a hard bluish black, rather than a jet black. The hair is very scanty and weak. The pigs are well shaped, and of high quality, but there is a general want of stamina about them; in fact, they have the appearance of being too finely bred. As in all finely bred animals the offal is small, and they come to maturity early. When crossed with the Berkshire, they gain in stamina and lose little in quality, becoming altogether a better general purpose pig, as the excessive proportion of fat is lessened.

The National Pig Keepers' Association have formulated no " standard of excellence " of the Small Black breed. There are a few small typical divergences between the Essex, Dorset, and Sussex strains, which render it somewhat difficult to bring all under one heading. The recognised features which are necessary in a breed in which early maturity, lightness of offal, and meat of fine quality, are particularly aimed at. Lightness of bone should not be carried so far that the legs will not support the body sufficiently to allow the animals to travel freely. Colour whole black, the skin being free from reddish or purplish tinge;

Fig. 5.—Essex Pig.

hair fine and plentiful; short head, not too small; nose short and turned up; ears short and erect; tail set on high; and the general appearance of a wide deep carcase, as described in the points of the Small White breed.

SECTION II.

SELECTION OF STOCK.

INFLUENCE OF DISTRICT.

The farmer when selecting cattle or sheep has to take into consideration the soil and climate of his farm, as stock which does well on one class of soil will not prosper on another. If he fancies a particular breed and desires to keep it, he must first be assured that it will adapt itself to the soil, or he will probably be disappointed. However, in the case of pigs he need trouble himself very little on this point. In only a few instances can the breeds be said to be in any way indigenous to the districts in which they are kept, and in all cases the breeds are strongly composed of foreign blood. He requires an animal of sufficiently strong constitution to thrive under the conditions in which it has to be kept, but he need not take into consideration the soil or the local breed. In selecting a breed one of the first considerations is colour—not because colour has a very important bearing on the thriving properties of the animal, but because it often greatly influences the sale. In some districts white pigs are practically unsaleable, while in others, often not far distant, no one will buy a black one. If it is expected that the animals will be sold locally, it is therefore necessary to consult the local taste. The preference for a particular colour has generally been brought about through some local pig breeder of repute having kept a particular breed which has spread through the district; these have been so much better than others less well bred that only those of the particular type have been regarded as profitable. Anyone can see the difference in colour, but it takes more skill to discern the good points in a young or lean pig, therefore colour has a greater influence on the sale than it ought to have. In the larger markets, where men are accustomed to see all breeds brought together, colour has little influence on the buyer, beyond being a little guide as to the quality of the meat. As a good horse may be of any colour, so a good pig cannot be of the wrong colour.

POPULAR TASTE.

The popular taste has greatly changed during the past few years, or perhaps it would be more accurate to say that the demand has changed, for one can hardly imagine anyone preferring coarse meat to that which is finely grained. Until comparatively recent years the "biggest was best" in pork. Now, however, there is little demand for big joints. Big fat joints are found to waste very much in cooking, while the grossness of the fat renders it distasteful to any but the strongest digestions. Pork was practically the only meat within the reach of the labouring and artisan classes before the importation of beef and mutton assumed the large proportions it has attained during the past twenty years, and they had little opportunity of choosing their joints. With better wages they have a larger choice, and the coarse meat which sold readily a few years ago is very difficult to dispose of. The increasing popularity of lightly cured bacon also tends towards the curing of smaller sides. Those enormous sides of bacon which made the rafters of the farmer's kitchen groan are almost useless to him, for the labourers will not eat it. Small joints of fresh pork are required to compete with fresh beef and mutton. Bacon curers are always glad of pigs weighing from 7 to 8 scores (of 20 lbs.). The larger firms show their appreciation of the small sides by giving the highest price for pigs of 7 to 8 scores, and by taking off 6d. per score until a uniform grossness is obtained. Everything therefore tends towards the production of joints of moderate size.

As bacon curers are prepared to pay the highest price for pigs of 8 scores, the typical pig should be one which is fit to kill at that weight. It must not be forgotten, however, that it costs less to produce a score of meat after the pig reaches 8 scores than it does before. There is proportionately less frame to build up, and less lean in proportion to fat is made. It costs less to produce fat than to build up frame and to make lean meat; so it is not necessarily correct to kill pigs at 8 scores. If, however, a pig is suitable to kill at that weight, or to be kept on to a larger weight, advantage may be taken of the condition of the market to dispose of it when the feeder thinks best. Speaking generally it is better that a pig will stand feeding to a considerably greater weight than 8 scores than that it should only exceed that weight by a small amount. An animal which under ordinary good feeding fattens to only about 8 scores within a reasonable time generally fattens too grossly, and consists of little more than blubber.

SELECTION IN ACCORDANCE WITH TASTE.

But selection of stock cannot be made entirely dependent on the highest price paid per pound; other points have to be brought into consideration. Breeders of high-class stock urge that the greatest profit is obtained from pigs when they are fed on as much rich food as they can consume from birth to slaughter. The farmer, however, has to consider the nature of the food he has at his disposal. This is often comparatively coarse and not suitable for fattening animals, but would be wasted if not consumed. Strong store pigs will consume it and turn it to profit, therefore it is not always wise to regard the pig as an animal that must be fattened on expensive foods from birth. A certain number of pigs can always be profitably kept on a farm more or less as scavengers, and the cottager often has a supply which can be turned to profitable account in a similar manner. When pigs are required to rough it they should be strong in constitution and lengthy in frame, so that when they are taken up to fatten they will make up to good weights. A distinction must be made between a big pig and a coarse one— it exists, though it is not always recognised. A large pig may possess quality throughout, as for instance a well-bred and well-fed Tamworth, which will give excellent meat; whereas a small pig, badly bred, will give coarse meat. The Large and the Middle White may be grown to heavy weights without gross coarseness and with little waste. As a rule where there is coarse food to be consumed the larger breeds are preferable. Where the food is in a concentrated form, smaller breeds should be kept. For general purposes the middle size pigs, the Middle Yorkshire and the Berkshire, are most suitable, because they may be made ready for the butcher at any age. The Large Yorkshire and the Tamworth are essentially bacon pigs, while the smaller breeds are more particularly porkers. This is not meant to convey a hard and fast rule, as good bacon is made from the smaller breeds, just as one sees excellent porkers from the larger breeds; but generally the view is correct.

VIGOROUS STOCK.

As a rule farmers find well-bred animals as suitable for their purposes as those which are absolutely pure bred, but it is advisable to keep a boar which is pure bred, so that inferior features in the general

stock may be rectified. The boar exerts a strong
influence on the offspring, particularly on the frame,
while the sow bequeaths the constitution. Highly-
bred stock, especially such as has for a long period
been subjected to the forced feedings which some
pedigree and show yard stock are put, render them
subject to various weaknesses unless great care is
exercised. To avoid this, strong well-bred sows
of good farm stocks, which have lived under more
natural conditions, are found serviceable. As a rule
the offspring are more numerous and more robust
than those where the parents are from pampered
stocks. It is, however, important the sow should be
well bred as well as robust. While developing
stock by crossing it is important to keep special
points in view, for though the first cross of pedigree stock almost always results in offspring of
greater merit than that of either parents, yet
subsequent crosses are frequently inferior. This is
the chief objection to breeding from stock which is not
pure on both sides. Careful observation and skill,
however, minimise the chances, and it is not
necessary that there should be any retrogression.
By selecting animals with good points and reselect-
ing from these, in course of time a new strain is
established in which the prominent features become
fixed; in fact, a new pedigree is established. Pigs
so soon feel the effect of better breeding that the
improvement of a breed is not an expensive process.
This helps to make pig breeding an interesting as
well as a profitable business, and anyone possessing
skill, a keen eye to the merits of an animal, should

endeavour to turn it to account. It is necessary to
understand the primary laws of breeding, to determine a standard at which to aim, and then to carefully
work to attain it.

THE VALUE OF POINTS.

The value of points of excellence as laid down
as a standard by those interested in the leading
breeds relates, of course, to pure bred animals such
as are suitable for show purposes. They are valuable also as indicating fixity of type, thus denoting
lengthy pedigree; nor can they be ignored by the
farmer in purchasing either boars to perpetuate the
breed, or breeding sows the stock of which he hopes
to improve.

Without dealing with the pig entirely as a show
animal, it is well to consider some of the features
which the Breeders' Association regard as indications
of excellence, for they convey much to the farmer
which is worthy of attention, while the mere state-
ment of the points may convey little that is
instructive to the amateur pig keeper, unless some
explanation is given. Taking the Large White breed
as an example—if the colour is not white it is
evident that there has been a cross with a black
breed within recent years, and the strain is therefore
not pure. While blue spots are objectionable, they
are traceable through some of the purest strains ; the
chief objection lies in that if they were freely
admitted it would leave the field too open to crossing, they are objected to as a safeguard. The head

is preferred moderately long and broad, because length often indicates length of frame, while breadth denotes thriving properties. Long fine ears denote fine breeding, the fringe of fine hair indicates that the coarse bristly hair of the old style of pig is eliminated. A fairly long neck is generally associated with growthiness. Chest wide and deep, generally goes with good girth through the heart, always a strong point in well-bred stock. Coarse open shoulders are not associated with a level frame, and the heart girth is generally spoiled by them. Straight legs, well set, indicate activity and vigour, besides materially helping the general shape of the animal. Short pasterns are best suited for carrying heavy weights, as are good strong feet. Back long and level, loin broad, sides deep, ribs well sprung, belly full, underline straight, flank thick and well let down, are essential to the perfection of the general form, and without them the pig lacks a meat-producing frame, and the sides of bacon are faulty. Quarters full, and hams broad and well let down to the hocks are necessary to the proper development of the hind quarters, and add materially to the animal's weight. Skin not too thick denotes good breeding and small waste. When free from wrinkles, careful and long continued good breeding is shown. A long thin tail is altogether in sympathy with the rest of the frame, but a coarse tail indicates want of breeding. Some of the old breeds of coarsest type were wrinkled in the skin, which sometimes hung in wattles. Many of these points are common to other breeds. In the Small White breed a diminutive pug nose is allowed, because it indicates what is wanted in it, an early maturity. In fact, everything about the head and neck is indicative of rapid feeding. Absolute black colour in the Berkshire indicates recent crossing with the Small Black breed. Black in the Tamworth suggests crossing with one of the black breeds.

DENTITION AS INDICATING AGE.

The modern highly developed state to which pigs have been brought has somewhat affected their dentition. The result is, the age of a pig cannot always be definitely estimated by the teeth. It can be approximated fairly closely, but as some show precocious dentition it is possible to pass off some of those as being older than they really are. In the same way those which show this early dentition are unfavourably placed in exhibitions, where the entries in particular classes are restricted to age as shown by dentition. Undoubtedly, many honest exhibitors showed animals which were eligible for entry under a certain age, but which showed dentition usually associated with pigs of a greater age. A danger was incurred, in that, as there was no other means of arriving at the age of the pigs except that of the word of the exhibitor, dishonest exhibitors were tempted to take advantage of the loophole afforded by this abnormal dentition, and showed pigs in classes which they were not in reality eligible for. The leading agricultural societies rightly decided that, to prevent unfair entries being made, a standard of dentition according to age should be decided upon, and that it should be abided by.

In that useful pamphlet on "Dentition as indicative of the Age of the Animals of the Farm," by Professor Brown, published by the Royal Agricultural Society, a section is devoted to pig dentition, in which are several illustrations indicating the age of pigs.

A full-mouthed pig has six incisor or single teeth in the front of both upper and lower jaw—two central, two lateral, and two corner teeth. Behind these are the four tusks, one on each side of both the upper and lower jaws. Between the tusks and the molar or double teeth there are usually four small teeth which are called pre-molars, one on each side of both jaws, and twenty-four molars, six on each side of the upper and lower jaws. At various stages the teeth undergo changes from birth to eighteen months, when the last molar comes through. At twenty months all teeth are well up.

At birth two small tusk-like teeth are found laterally placed in each jaw, leaving an open space in the front of the mouth. There are then no molars or other teeth showing.

At one month these temporary molars are cut on each side of the jaw, top and bottom. The second and third are well up, the first just coming through the gum. Two central incisors are cut in each jaw.

At two months the temporary central incisors are fully developed. The gum shows signs that the lateral temporary incisors will soon come through. The first temporary molar is level with the second.

At three months the temporary set of teeth is complete. The temporary corner teeth are further removed from each other, owing to the growth of the jaw. From three to five months no fresh teeth appear. At five months there are signs of cutting of the pre-molars. The fourth molar, which is seen behind the temporary teeth, is evidently shortly coming through.

At six months the wolf teeth, between the tusk and the pre-molars, appear; also the third permanent molars.

At nine months the corner permanent teeth are well up, and the permanent tusks may be up   If the permanent tusks are well developed the pig is over nine months.

At one year the central permanent incisors are expected to be cut, but not up. Often, however, the temporary incisors are still in their place. The fifth molar is cut at from ten to twelve months, so it should be well up at a year.

Shortly after a year the three anterior molars disappear, at fifteen months are replaced by the three anterior permanent molars. At seventeen or eighteen months the sixth molar is cut, and the lateral temporary incisors generally give place to the permanent.

At twenty months all the teeth are well up. The sixth molar stands quite free from contact with the angle of the jaw. The other molars show signs of wear. The age subsequently cannot be definitely fixed; and even at the ages mentioned some latitude must be allowed for precocious dentition.

SELECTION OF THE BOAR.

It is a law of breeding that an animal which has been for a long time bred on definite lines, so that its characteristic features have been perpetuated unbrokenly through several generations, makes a great impression on the offspring from animals which have been bred less carefully. The influence is proportionately greater as the un-pedigreed stock is less well bred. This is one of the great advantages of pedigree. The better bred animal is said to be prepotent. Again, the male is as a rule more prepotent than the female, at any rate so far as the size and quality are concerned. The advantage, therefore, of using a boar which is possessed of good pedigree is easily understood. It is fortunate the boar is prepotent, because the boar can be made to influence a large herd, whereas the sow's influence only goes so far as her own offspring are concerned. For this reason special attention should be given to the selection of the boar. The offspring are to take his shape and form. If he is long on the leg, thin in the forequarter, narrow in the loin, covered with hard bristles in the place of fine hair, and coarse in bone, it is certain that his offspring will turn out badly. These features belong to the unimproved animal, or at any rate prove that he has not been subjected to improvement for a long time. Such a pig is not far removed from the wild pig, and he will neither rest nor thrive. A thick neck is not valuable so much for the meat it carries as it is as a proof that it is of a thriving disposition. The sides should be deep and long with thick flesh. The flank should be full, giving a good straight underline. The ribs should be well sprung from the backbone, and the loin should be broad. The back should be straight, tending rather to arch than to dip. The legs should be full, with the meat well down to hocks. The bone from the hock should be fine. In highly-bred pigs this has been so much reduced in size as to appear almost out of proportion to the size of the animal; but it is a valuable characteristic, as it denotes lightness of offal. The ears should be fine, as thick ears denote coarseness of skin generally. The tail should be well set on and not too coarse. The skin should be well covered with fine hair, as this usually denotes a hardy constitution and a thin skin; hard bristles are objectionable. The skin should not be in folds or wattles. Viewed from the side or from behind the general appearance should be that of fulness, all parts being well developed, so as to show evenness of contour and outline., The almost indescribable appearance of quality suggesting fine meat throughout must not be wanting, but it is important that the boar has a masculine character, and does not lack robustness.

THE SOW.

The features desirable in a boar are as a rule necessary in the sow, but she should be of more feminine character. Her chief duty is to produce young and be able to support them. It is therefore important that she is provided with sufficient teats to supply her young with milk. She requires a teat

for each pig, as they feed at one time; if there is not
a teat for each the weakest get no food. It is
therefore of little use to have a pig without a teat
to suckle. A sow should possess at least twelve
teats. Small litters are not profitable. The sow
has to be kept in an unprofitable condition for as
long a time before farrowing a small litter as she
does before producing a big one. A sow can rear
twelve pigs without being overtaxed, provided she
is fairly well fed. The aim should be to produce
big litters, and as a rule sows with a large number
of teats have greater fecundity than those with few.
A specially good sow may possess fewer teats, and
it may be desirable to breed from her. The small
number of teats need not prevent her from being
bred from, but only those of her offspring should be
kept which have a greater number. In course of a
few generations the number of teats may be increased
if selection in this respect is carefully carried out,
and there will be little trouble in keeping up the
required number. It is advisable to cross a sow
with a deficiency of teats with a boar from a prolific
mother.

It is important that the sow should be well
tempered, or she will prove intractable at the time
of farrowing, and will probably contract the highly
objectionable habit of killing and eating her young.
Eating little pigs is a characteristic which sometimes
runs in families, and if it is persisted in there is no
other method than to get rid of the breed and get in
a new stock. Temper and other constitutional characteristics of the sow are largely reproduced in the

offspring, so they must be taken into consideration when selecting the sow. It is therefore advisable to know as much as possible about the sow before purchasing her. A risk is always run when buying in from an open market. It is natural that those who possess sows with faults which are only apparent at the time of farrowing should be desirous of avoiding trouble to themselves, therefore there is always a large proportion of those sold which possess peculiarities which are of an undesirable nature. The habit of eating the young is one of the most frequent causes for getting rid of a sow. Small litters is another. Want of sufficient milk to rear the young is a very frequent one, as is also a liability to milk fever. Inversion of the uterus is occasionally the cause. Laziness and carelessness on the part of the sow, whereby she does not take reasonable precautions to prevent her from lying on her young and suffocating them, is a habit some sows acquire, though this can generally be guarded against by keeping her from getting too fat, and by placing a protective rail round the sty so as to afford a chance of escape for the little pigs. All these add to the risk of purchasing in the open market, and there is beyond this the danger of infectious diseases, which is by no means a small one. It is advisable, therefore, to increase the stock on the farm by breeding, obtaining the necessary change of blood through the boar, which should be bought from the hands of those who exercise greatest care in the management of their stock. Those who require to purchase sows should take every precaution so that they know what they are buying. It may be taken that those who possess sows of exceptional merit will keep them in preference to those which are not so valuable as breeders. A certain amount of risk is run in buying yilts, or maiden sows, but if they are from good strains, and the mother is of good disposition, it may be reasonably supposed that the offspring partakes of her disposition and general character.

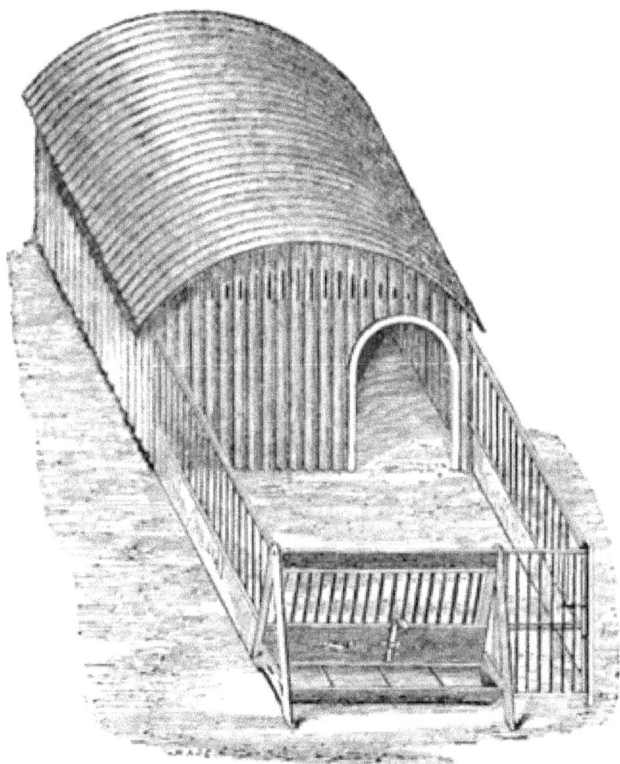

IRON PIGGERY. FIG. 6.

SECTION III.

HOUSING.

ECONOMY IN BUILDING STIES.

The housing of the pigs is a matter of no small importance. On it (especially in the case of young pigs) depends the success with which they will be kept. It is by no means necessary to build princely piggeries. The amount of money spent on a piggery is not an absolute guide as to its value for the purposes of pig rearing; there are expensively built sties where pigs prosper but little, and others which cost little where pigs always thrive. In days of great agricultural prosperity money was too often spent as an advertisement to the architect; perhaps princely homesteads tempted tenants to take farms at a price beyond what they were worth; but undoubtedly in many instances money was wastefully expended. We do not advise extravagant expenditure in the construction of sties. Many of the so-called labour-saving methods and appliances are so in a very small degree. Warmth, ventilation, room for exercise, and good flooring are the requisites.

CONDITIONS ENSURING WARMTH AND COMFORT.

Warmth is obtained by the use of stout building material, a sheltered but sunny position, and a dry floor. The pig revels iu warmth, and when left to itself will seek it by burrowing into the heated manure of the farmyard. Cold affects it prejudicially; and it turns to profitable account only a portion of the food supplied, as an extra share has to go to maintain the bodily heat of the animal. If the place is very cold the pig becomes chilled, aud the lungs frequently become affected. Stout walls of brickwork or masonry afford the most even temperature. A thatched roof is coolest in summer and warmest in winter, and under it pigs thrive better than under any other kind of roofing. The danger of fire is the chief objection, and this of course is a small one wheu the percentage of firings is considered; while if the place is insured even this objection is overcome. The necessity of somewhat frequent repair and occasional untidiness cause it to be unpopular, but where the raising of pigs is the matter of first consideratiou there is no doubt that thatch is the best roof for the pigs to live under. Slates are very susceptible to change of temperature, and the sty is cold in winter and hot in summer if the roof is not boarded as well. The double roof of slates and boards is objectionable, as it affords harbourage for rats. Tiles form a fairly equable roof, being only moderately affected by changes of temperature. Galvanised irou and zinc are even less suitable than slates. Where used, a layer of straw should be placed beneath to act as a non-conductor to heat. They are then serviceable, and form a cheap roofing.

Pigs require to bask in sunshine occasionally, but they suffer from being exposed too long to the burning rays of a summer sun : a means of escape to shelter should be provided. A southerly aspect is most suitable in those cases where the sty and the exercise court are built in one—the sty being under a roof, and the court communicating with it by means of a doorway. A range of sties built along the side of a barn with a sunny aspect are always warm. Taking into consideration the cost of building the sties and the actual requirements of pigs, the lean-to sty is the best; and (unless a loft is built over the sty) it is wasteful beyond the endurance of modern profits to build the expensive wide-roofed piggeries about which so much has been written. In all farm buildings feeding passages are more or less a luxury; the saving of time in feeding is not so great as is commonly stated. The high front of the manger in cattle-sheds causes almost as much loss of time to the feeder as he gains in being able to walk in front of the animals instead of behind them. Having had experience in both, we would certainly not go to the expense of building a cattle-shed required to contain a feeding passage, a cattle-stall, and a passage behind for mucking out. In piggeries the same holds good. Buildings can easily be arranged to allow feeding to be done from the outside. The only occasion where they are reasonably permissible—having in view cost and utility—is when a double row of sties are formed along a central passage. The cost of a building is so much regulated by the width of roof it has to carry that this point should never be lost sight of.

PRINCIPAL FEATURES OF PIGGERIES.

It is not necessary that the sty be high. So long as a man can stand up in it to throw out the dung, and perform any other ordinary work, nothing more is required. A lean-to roof five feet high in front (with a gradual rise, according to the material used in covering the roof) is sufficient. The same applies when a double row is built back to back. This form is suitable as division between two yards. A double row of this kind is built with only one back wall, thus lessening the cost. In these, as well as in the lean-to sty, the important work of mucking-out must be done from the front. It is always advisable to have a court before each sty, though where the farmyard is intended to act as a court it may be dispensed with, as the pigs may get their exercise there. In sties of this type, feeding must naturally be done from the outside. This is not difficult now, as feeding shutes which can be fixed into the wall are easily obtainable; or the modern iron feeding trough with flapping front may be used. This can be built in, so as to form part of the wall. A great advantage in feeding the animals in the exercise court is that the wash is not spilt or slopped about the living chamber, which consequently keeps drier and sweeter. The exercise court is often dispensed with where store pigs or barren sows occupy the sties. The feeding is then done in a common trough placed in a convenient position. It answers all reasonable requirements in such cases, except where the pigs differ much in size, as the smallest get the worst chance of feeding.

The best means of communication between the living chamber and the exercise court is a flapping door, hanging and swinging from the top in such a way that the pig can pass either in or out at will, a trick it soon learns. A bolt should be attached, so that the door can be fixed when desired. A disadvantage to the out-of-door feeding is that the food gets cold in winter. However, as the feeding should be regulated so that only so much is given as will be cleared up at a meal, this is not a matter of greatest importance. It should rather tend towards promoting careful feeding.

Proper ventilation should be provided by means of vents in the roof, assisted by a small closing lattice high in the wall. It is not advisable that the air should sweep the floor of the inner chamber, as that creates a cold draught about the pigs. The air should circulate over the pigs, when the impure gases and smells will be taken away, and the sty will not be too cold.

CONSTRUCTION OF PIGGERIES.

Piggeries may be elaborated to almost any extent, but very often a larger amount is spent on making some improvement which will assist the feeder than will add to the comfort and well-being of the pigs. Where expense need not be considered this does not matter, but such cases are the exception. The most simple form of sty is that where an open-fronted building is provided with a small yard or court. This, however, is not so comfortable as one where the front is built up, except a small opening to provide a doorway for ingress and egress, as an open front is naturally most subject to atmospheric changes. A typical sty—which, if several are built side by side, makes a range of piggeries—gives a section similar to that shown in Fig. 7. When one

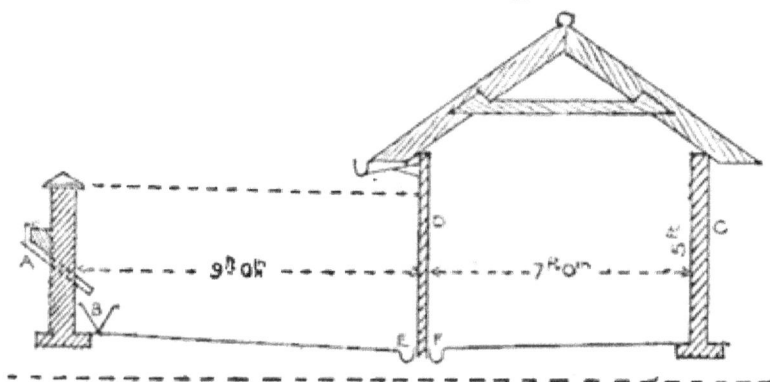

FIG. 7.

only is built it is suitable for those who keep but one sow or a few store pigs. The court answers as an exercise and feeding yard. A sty of 7 ft. by 7 ft. and a court 9 ft. by 7 ft. is a convenient size for general purposes. The floors require laying at a slight incline to carry off wet, but if the food is given to the animals in the court very little wet will get into the sty. The food may be poured through a shute (A) to a feeding trough (B). When built in brick the back wall may be 9 in. thick, and the front wall $4\frac{1}{2}$ in. It is better to make the front wall 9 in., and at any rate the first foot from the floor should be of that thickness. The back wall should be 5 ft. high, the front about 5 ft. 4 in., so as to allow for the fall of the floor. Drains placed at E and F will carry off wet. They should be open except against the doorway, where they should be covered, otherwise the animals carry a lot of wet on to their bed.

Good temporary sties are built of timber, and nothing is cheaper or more effective than disused railway sleepers. To prevent cold from getting through, they may be used double, each layer breaking joint with the other; or the joints, where the single thickness is adopted, should be made airtight by a strip of lath nailed over them. A sow requires a sty of at least 7 ft. by 7 ft. For general farm purposes, where breeding and fattening are carried on, a sty 10 ft. by 10 ft. is a very useful size. Ample room is given to the sow at breeding, and when she no longer requires to be shut up, it is large enough to hold a strong lot of fattening pigs. Where a court is attached to a sty of this description it is not needed for the fattening pigs, and may be used as a pen for the sow at night, or at any time it is desired to keep her shut up.

Adapting Existing Building to Piggeries.

The profit attaching to the rearing of pigs varies very considerably from time to time, and occasionally it is expedient to increase the stock beyond the capacity of the piggeries. Good accommodation may be obtained by adapting barns to the purpose of the piggery. We know a barn thus adapted, which for a long time has held from twenty to thirty sows and litters. The fittings in this are very simple: stout slatted hurdles form the only divisions, the separate sties are arranged along the walls, which leaves an open feeding court and exercise ground for the young pigs. As the building is enclosed, and thus protected from cold, there is no need of brick divisions, even where the building is turned into a permanent piggery. When adapting a barn to a piggery, where permanence and appearance are considerations, the following plan may be adopted:—To render it suitable for fattening pigs, as well as for breeding sows and their young, sties 10 ft. by 8 ft. may be taken; but if intended only for sows, smaller sties are sufficient, though (as a breeding rail is necessary) it is well to keep them up to 8 ft. by 8 ft., especially as the sow has to feed in the sty, and not in a court.

By arranging the sties along the outside of the building, a common feeding court for the little pigs is provided, which is also convenient as an exercise pen. In the accompanying rough sketch, which may be altered according to requirements or the shape of the barn, sties 10 ft. by 8 ft. are shown. Around the outsides, about 9 in. from the walls, and 9 in. in height, a bar is placed, so that the little pigs may get away from their mother in case she falls on them, which would be impossible and fatal should they be lying close to the wall. The front of the sty is filled up by a top bar, 3 ft. 6 in. from the ground at the top; and below, 6 ft. in length and 2 ft. 3 in. in height, are occupied by a feeding-trough, made with a swinging board, which may be fixed at the front or back of the trough as desired, so that the pigs may be kept back

from or allowed to get to their food according to the
wish of the feeder. The remaining space, 2 ft., is
occupied by a doorway, which is constructed so as
to answer several purposes. It is the doorway into
the sty, whereby the sow can enter, and also through
which the manure can be taken out. The lower
half is made after the principle of a lamb hurdle,
which allows the little ones to run out while the
mother remains within. As it may be desirable not
to let the little pigs out at times, a hinged board
should be attached, so that it can be made to cover
the openings at will.

The floor of the pens should be made to slope
towards the feeding-trough, so that any liquid may
run away from the bedding, and pass under the
trough into a gutter, J, and be conveyed out of the
piggery. The court B should also slope slightly
towards the gutters.

The spaces C C D may be utilised for bins to hold
meal, roots, &c., and as a mixing house; and, if
desired, a steamer or copper may be set up for
cooking food. Thus, all the requirements of a
piggery are compactly placed under one cover. The
doors may be placed as is found most convenient
for the particular situation. There are many
instances where those shown would be convenient,
as (E) outside door into stackyard, (F) hand-gate
into court, and (G) doorway into yard to allow the
sows an exit, and as an opening through which the
dung might be dragged into the yard.

In these days, when so much land is going out
of cultivation and the cropping is so much altered,

PLAN OF BARN ADAPTED AS A PIGGERY FOR
BREEDING AND FATTENING PIGS. (*Not made to Scale.*)

FIG. 8.

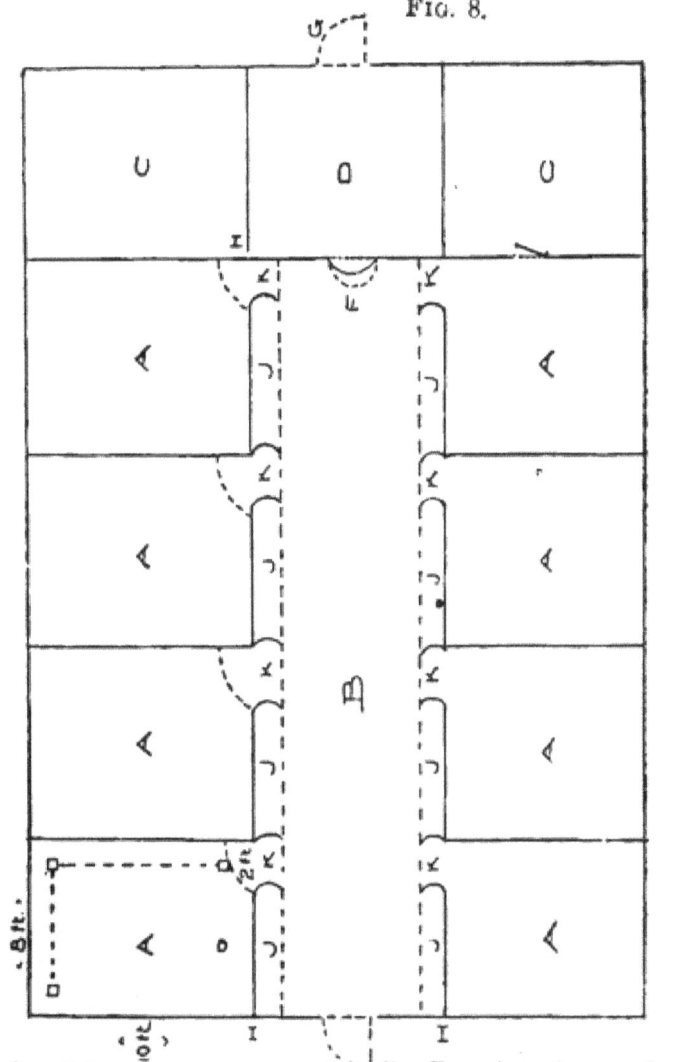

A A. Sties.
  B. Small pig court.
C C. Meal and root stores.
  D. Mixing-house.
  F. Hand gate to court.

G. Door into farmyard.
H. Feeding trough.
J. Drainage gutter.
K. Archway over gutter.

E

barns available as piggeries may often be obtained,
and thus turned to profitable account. As the

FRONT ELEVATION OF A STY.—Fig. 9.

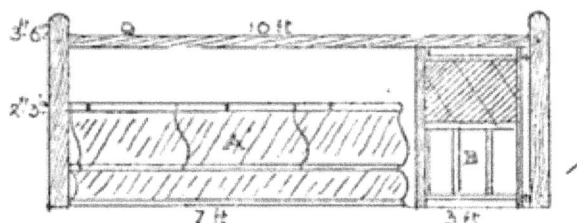

A. Fixed trough, with a swinging board attached to the bar
    at the top.
B. Hand gate opening inwards. Lower portion, with open-
    ings to allow the little pigs to go to and from the court.
C. Top of feeding trough.
D. Top rail.

animals are entirely under cover there is not much
trouble as to drainage.

FLOORING OF THE STY.

The flooring of the sty is an important feature,
on it in no small degree depends the healthiness of
the pigs. Cold floors are the source of chills, rheumatism, and many other ailments, while foul floors
give rise to many diseases. It is important that
the floor is one that can be swilled down with water
occasionally, for this reason it must be hard; at the
same time it must not be too slippery, as there is
danger of injury. Asphalt, cement, and other sub-
stances have been recommended from time to time,

but taking one thing with another, hard and impervious bricks, laid in cement, are best. However, these are cold, and it is necessary to protect the pigs from coming into direct contact with them, at any rate in that portion where they make their bed. Nothing is better for this than a movable slatted or sparred rack covering about half the sty. It should be made sufficiently light for the attendant to be able to rear it on end, so that he may sweep away any accumulation of dirt or moisture that may have gathered on the bricks, and also so that he may brush off anything that has collected on it. As wood is absorbent it should be dressed with pitch tar, and when through age or use it shows signs of absorbing liquid, it should be well scoured and re-coated. The rack should be made of slats 3 in. by 1 in., nailed an inch apart to battens about 3 in. thick, so that moisture may pass through to the bricks and run unimpeded to the drains. The rack should be kept covered with fresh straw.

Liquid Manure from Slatted Floors.

Sparred floors covering the whole sty have been adopted in some instances. In this case there is an objection that if the sty is not kept well littered too much dung passes through into the tank placed below. This is a serious loss, for one of the chief advantages of pig keeping is the manure obtained from it. The dung and urine should mix with litter so as to form farmyard manure. Of course, the manurial value of manure in a liquid condition is as great as when it is absorbed by straw, but the mechanical effect of the manure is lost, and it is this characteristic which renders farmyard manure valuable beyond other manures chemically equally good. It is contended by some advocates of this type of flooring that it is not necessary to use any straw whatever, as on the boards the pigs lie sufficiently clean and dry. For the sake of the pigs, however, there can be little doubt that they are more comfortable and thrive better where they get clean sweet bedding in addition. Where no litter is given the manure is very concentrated, and possesses little advantage over the ordinary concentrated artificial manures.

The situation of the sty is important. It is well that it lies sufficiently high for the drainage to be got rid of easily, and the openings should have a southerly aspect, so that they may have the advan of sun, and be sheltered from cold winds.

· In summer time store pigs thrive better when allowed to run out in a cool yard than when kept too closely confined, particularly if the sty is hot.

FITTINGS OF STY.

The fittings of the sty are very simple. Practically all that is wanted is a feeding trough. Small pigs naturally require smaller troughs than do bigger pigs. Iron troughs are preferable to wooden ones, because they are more easily cleaned. Wooden troughs absorb a portion of the liquid food, and become stale and sour, affecting more or less injuriously the fresh food placed in them. Circular troughs with numerous divisions are very useful for feeding young pigs. The partitions keep the younger and weaker ones from being shoved aside.

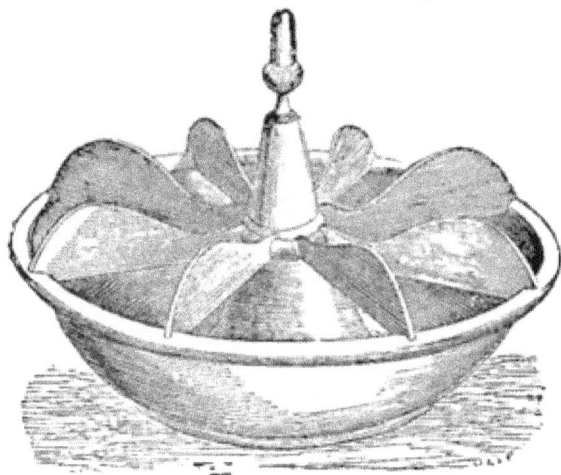

CIRCULAR TROUGH.   FIG. 10.

The trough may be made to form part of the front of the sty when one of the type shown in Fig. 9 is used.   They are so very convenient for filling and

IRON TROUGH.   FIG. 11.

feeding from that their adoption is rapidly spreading. Sows are very liable to upset light troughs, and it is an advantage to use those which are fixed. It is necessary to have the food in a convenient position, so that time is not wasted in getting it to the pigs.

If the ordinary store-houses are not conveniently placed for this purpose, a small portion of the building should be set apart and fitted with bins to hold the food, and a cistern or tank be provided to

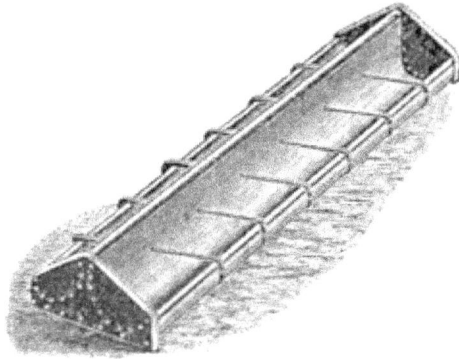

IRON TROUGH WITH DOUBLE SIDES. FIG. 12.

hold the wash. Where potatoes or roots are fed a boiler is necessary to cook them. This may take the form of a fixed boiler, or a portable one may be got which will answer the purpose admirably. A

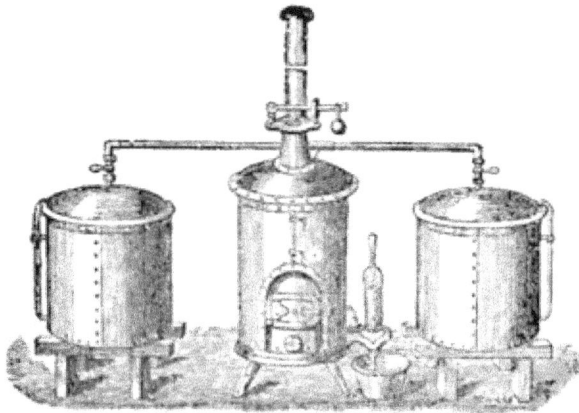

STEAMER AND BOILER FOR COOKING. FIG. 13.

combined boiler and steamer is a convenient form, and on a farm has many uses. Where few pigs are kept there is no necessity for any special boiler, and potatoes may be cooked over the kitchen fire. Hot water for warming food, when necessary, can be got from the same source. Under ordinary circumstances there is not great gain in cooking food, except potatoes, as most of the benefits derived from it can be obtained by heating the food with warm water.

COOKING POTATOES.

Potatoes are distinctly indigestible, and their full feeding properties are not utilised unless they are cooked. Although diseased potatoes smell badly when they are cooked, there is nothing injurious in them provided they are properly cleaned. As they smell badly they are an inconvenience about the house, and it is then an out-of-door furnace or a boiling-house is useful. The best form of potato cleaner, suitable also for cleaning mangels or turnips, is a cylinder made of slats placed about an inch apart round a frame. Inside the cylinder guides placed helically, or corkscrew-wise, from end to end to conduct the potatoes from the mouth to the outlet, are necessary. A spindle carrying a handle at one end, to make the whole concern revolve, must be run through the centre. The bottom of the cylinder should set in a trough containing water. The motion through the water, together with the rolling of the potatoes themselves, well frees them from dirt. A more

simple potato washer can be made by placing a
slatted wooden rack in a trough ; this should very
nearly fit, but should be small enough to float.
Potatoes should be placed in the trough and water
be poured in ; the rack with potatoes will float, and
if these are well rubbed with a whalebone brush or
a common besom, the cleaning will be quickly
effected. The dirt will fall through the openings
in the rack, leaving the clean potatoes on the top.
A small quantity of water will wash a great many
potatoes, as the trough need only be cleaned out
when the accumulation of dirt is so great as to impede
the work.

An advantage in boiling diseased potatoes is that
the fungus within them is killed, and can no longer
produce or carry on disease. Potato disease is
largely carried on from year to year by the fungus
within the diseased tuber, so this should be guarded
against—there is no more effectual way of effecting
this than by boiling. Potatoes should be kept
fresh when cooked. After cooking, the moisture
should be allowed to drain away, and after this the
potatoes should be mashed and placed in an airtight receptacle. If they are rammed in tightly so
that no air gets to them, they will keep fresh for a
considerable time. By taking off a layer daily no
mould will form, and the food will be wholesome. If
put loosely into a tub, and not compressed, they soon
become mouldy and unsafe to feed, at any rate to
young pigs.

SECTION IV.

FOODS.

FARM OFFAL.

Almost anything produced on the farm is suitable for pig food, or can be utilised for the pig's benefit. If one kind of grain is too heating, it can be moderated by being mixed with another more starchy; or if too starchy, it can be rendered more complete by the addition of one which is more nitrogenous. The green crops — clover, grass, potatoes, cabbages, vetches, mangels, &c. — have great value as pork producers; the waste products of the dairy are turned to excellent account; while the straw adds to the comfort and well-being of the animals, and by absorbing the dung, becomes valuable again as manure. Small quantities of foods which the more fastidious cattle will not eat are not allowed to waste; so that altogether the pig is a necessary adjunct to the farm.

It is urged by some recognised authorities that it is more profitable to force the feeding of pigs, and bring them to a rapid maturity, than to allow them to act as scavengers on the farm. We think, however, there is always room for a number of scavenging pigs on the farm, to clear up what would otherwise be wasted. It is certain that on all farms there is food worth far less than a pound, for most of it would not be consumed otherwise, which when fed by pigs produces far more than a pound's worth of meat, or frame on which to place the meat. On a smaller scale, the gardener and allotment holder has residues from crops which can be utilised in the growing of pigs, which (together with house refuse) make pig keeping a more profitable pursuit than it would be had all the food to be bought. We are personally not at all inclined to give up the idea of the pig as an animal which under some circumstances may be run as a store before being put up to fatten. It would be as wise to give up the idea as it would be to run no store cattle because it is found profitable to keep cattle at high pressure from birth to turn them out fat at twenty months to two years. There is room for both styles of feeding. What is most important is to feed the various foods to the best profit, and when buying to purchase those foods which give the best return.

BARLEY.

All cereals are exceedingly valuable as pig food, but barley is the best. Barley meal has long been looked upon as the most important concentrated food, and in experiments the opinion formed during long experience has been confirmed. Pigs keep in a healthy condition, the meat is of good quality, and great weight of meat is obtained from a given quantity. When arranging a diet for pigs the foods should be made to give an analytical value very similar to barley, as the proportion of albuminoids, fats, and carbohydrates in barley is that which is found to be most suitable for the production of pork. An excess in the proportion of albuminoids beyond those in barley does not give a profitable return. except in the case of young and growing pigs, which have to devote a considerable portion of the digested food to the building up of the frame. The nitrogen in barley of average quality is 1·65 per cent., the mineral matter 2·2, phosphoric acid 0·75, potash 0·55, carbohydrates 57·5, and oils 1·7.

The paper by Sir John Lawes and Sir John Gilbert which appeared in a recent number of the *Journal of the Royal Agricultural Society* draws attention to a paper in Vol. XIV. of the same journal, which gave a detailed report on a series of experiments carried out by them more than forty years ago. This was a very complete series, and no experiments carried out since have added much light on the subject. A large number of combinations of foods were tried, but barley was shown to be the best food; and those combinations of foods which approached nearest to it followed it closest. Barley is so easily assimilated by pigs that this point gave it an advantage over other foods analytically of the same value. To those interested in pig feeding the report on these experiments is especially valuable, and they would do well to study it.

BARLEY MEAL.

Barley should, as a rule, be ground before being given to pigs. A small quantity of whole grain thrown to young pigs occupies them, and appears to do them good. When barley is ground it should be well soaked before being consumed, as it is then even more digestible. Mixed with whey, wash, or water, it makes an easily digested food. The quantity of liquid to meal is generally regulated by the condition of the animal; for young pigs and stores it is given thin, but to fattening pigs it is gradually increased in consistency, so that when the animals are nearly fat it is a thick paste. When given in the concentrated form to fat pigs, care should be taken to stir it thoroughly. When given to show animals it is frequently mixed with milk and made into balls.

It is important that barley meal is sweet. When ground in a moist condition it rapidly heats in the bin, and is dangerous as food for young pigs, though less hurtful to stronger ones. Heated or fermented meal should not be given to sows which are suckling, as the milk is very liable to be affected, causing scour and other ailments to the little pigs. Barley should be dry when ground, as it is then less likely to ferment afterwards. Freshly-ground meal will often upset little pigs. It should be allowed to cool before being used, so that the heat generated by friction in the process of grinding may be lost, as this heat is productive of fermentation within the stomachs of the young pigs.

Whatever meal is given to pigs it is advisable to have two bins, so that a fresh lot of meal has not to be shot on to the remains of an older lot. The meal at the bottom of the bin is that most likely to ferment, and if this is left for a long time it gets mouldy and contaminates that placed above it. Meal worms also collect in it, and set up fermentation. The bin should therefore be thoroughly scraped out before a fresh supply is placed in it.

PURCHASING MEAL AND CORN.

English barley is generally preferred to foreign, because it is cleaner. Foreign samples often contain much dirt, and occasionally seeds of weeds which act injuriously on the pigs. It should be thoroughly cleaned, when the feeding value is very similar to the English-grown. The value of a sample of barley for feeding is chiefly regulated by weight. A sample of good, sound, dry barley weighs naturally 52 to 56 lbs. per imperial bushel, and the nearer it approaches this the better; if it is many pounds under it will cut little meal, but will largely consist of indigestible husk. A bushel of grain is that which, poured into a bushel measure, falls naturally into it without a jar of any sort, and is then struck off level with the top of the measure. If the vessel which holds the grain is allowed to rest on the bushel, or to knock it, or if the bushel receives a blow of any sort, a larger quantity of grain goes to the bushel, and it appears to be heavier, and therefore more valuable, than it actually is. Of course when buying by measure this does not matter, but it is a very foolish man who buys such stuffs as grinding barley or oats by measure.

As in all businesses there are men who are honest and those who are not, so are there honest and dishonest mealmen and millers. When buying meal the inexperienced and, only in a less degree, the experienced pig keeper is to a great extent dependent on the honesty of the seller. Thin kernelled, husky, damp barley when ground becomes barley meal just as much as when the best barley is used, but the actual value of one may not be half that of the other, therefore it is important to deal with a man of honesty. When sending barley to be ground the miller's honesty has to be trusted that the meal returned is actually made from the barley sent to him. So find an honest miller. We have known dishonest millers and dishonest mealmen, so we give the warning. Others have had the same experience, and it is for this reason that many prefer to grittle their barley at home.

CORN GRINDER, OR GRITTLER. FIG. 14.

The illustration shows a corn grinding mill suitable for a farm. Smaller grinders, costing £2 and upwards, are very serviceable for small holders.

The most glaring impertinence in the way of cheating on the part of the miller which has come under our notice was where cheap barley was mixed with maize sent to be ground, maize then being worth the exceptionally high price of 38s. per quarter. He could hardly have expected to escape detection, as the barley husk was so plainly visible. A sack of four bushels of barley cuts about five bushels of meal, and it is important to see that the full weight sent to the mill is returned.

OATS, WHEAT, AND MAIZE.

Oats are proportionately dear as compared with oats and maize at the present time, but when weight for weight they are about the same price they are very profitable for use as pig food. Oats should not weigh less than 38 lbs. per imperial bushel, and are more valuable as they increase in weight. They are especially valuable for young pigs, and for sows in milk, as they increase the flow of milk. They should not be given to sows during the last week before weaning, as they tend to excite the flow, and it is desirable to check rather than increase it at this time. Oats are easily digested, and contain rather more nitrogen than barley, they are therefore considered somewhat heating for pigs which are being fattened rapidly. They mix well with potatoes and maize, and the heating properties may be neutralised by a few mangels or other vegetables. Wheat is at present a cheap feeding stuff; in fact the cheapest. It weighs from 60 lbs. to 63 lbs. per imperial bushel. A sack of barley weighs 18 stones.

and a sack of wheat 19 stones, therefore when the price per sack is equal there is a gain of a stone in favour of wheat, which more than counterbalances the difference in feeding value, which is not great. It is considered slightly more heating than barley, but in a mixed diet this is easily corrected. Personally we have very little objection to a corn diet of wheatmeal, though a mixed diet is preferable. It mixes well with maize and potatoes.

Maize is a cheap food, and is very largely used, particularly in America. It weighs 60 lbs. per imperial bushel. When fed by itself it is too starchy, especially for young pigs. One of the characteristics of the experiments mentioned in connection with barley is deserving of special notice. The pigs fed on a diet of maize, with nothing but water additionally, throve remarkably during the first fortnight, presumably because the blood contained constituents which amalgamated with the somewhat one-sided starchy nature of the maize; afterwards, however, they fell back in condition, became sickly, and abscesses broke out on them, showing plainly that the food was not a complete one and did not supply the constituents necessary for the healthy growth and increase of the animals.

This should be a good object lesson for pig keepers. When maize is fed in conjunction with other more nitrogenous foods it is a highly profitable food. In America, where the pigs are largely fed on maize, the fat is very excessive and the flesh generally coarse and wasteful in cooking. However, they are kept in a healthy thriving condition by the grass or clover with which they are supplied. The green food supplies nitrogen and acts medicinally on the pigs, keeping them in a healthy condition and improving the quality of the meat. Maize is very hard and difficult to grind on stones, which it soon wears down. It is better not to give maize whole, though it is only necessary to grittle it finely. When given in wash it should be soaked for a considerable time. Maize should not be fed with potatoes, as the starchy proportions are increased, but should be given with oats, peas, beans, lentils, and other nitrogenous foods.

PEAS, BEANS, AND RICE MEAL.

Peas and beans are very similar in their nature, and are valuable as correctives to too starchy diets. The chief objection to them is that if given in large quantities for a lengthy period the meat, especially the lean, becomes very hard. A few mixed with other foods just before selling are an advantage, as they make the flesh firmer. Show pigs are improved by them in the same way, as they handle better when they have received a few. It is not desirable, however, to give them in large quantities. They may be ground to meal and stirred well in wash, but as a rule they are given whole. When boiled they are very palatable and easily digested. New peas and beans are somewhat indigestible, in fact there are portions of their constituents which require to undergo chemical changes before they can be assimilated by animals.

F

The changes are undergone slowly but naturally, and in the course of a year, when they are what is known as old peas or beans, they are far more valuable than when new. It is wasteful to consume new peas or beans; but the virtue of a good old bean has long been recognised.

Rice meal is often so cheap as to be well worth buying for feeding. It is essentially a starchy food, and should be corrected in the same manner as maize. It is easy of digestion, and suitable as pig food.

BRAN.

Bran, dan, pollard, middlings, seconds, and many other terms used more or less locally are names by which the offal or skin of wheat freed from flour in milling is known. The terms denote more or less one and the same thing, though bran is usually used to indicate a coarser material than dan or pollard. The present roller system of milling clears the skin from flour more thoroughly than is done on stones, and the proportion of albumioids in it are slightly increased, while the carbohydrates are materially decreased. Bran contains $3\frac{1}{2}$ per cent. of oil, which is beneficial as a food, and also helps to keep the bowels in a healthy condition. Well-soaked bran is an excellent food for sows after pigging, and for young pigs; indeed, when the price is low it is profitable for feeding pigs of all ages. It, however, fluctuates considerably, but may be considered a cheap food, even as prices for other foods run, at about £3 10s. per ton.

Finer divisions of bran, such as pollards, mix better with water, as they contain rather more meal and the flakes of skin are smaller.

ACORNS AND BEECH MAST.

Acorns are a good pig food, but they should be well ripened, and it is better for them to be stored, when they become more digestible and more nutritious. They are more profitably fed when they are consumed with other food, rather than as a whole diet. In districts where acorns are abundant it is decidedly wasteful not to utilise them. Strong stores are required for the purpose of running out to pick them up. They will not get fat in the process, but will grow strong frames on which meat can be laid cheaply subsequently. When running out they get other food as well, as they eat almost any green stuff that comes in their way. It is important, however, that they get a plentiful supply of water. With other feeding stuffs so cheap, acorns are not worth many pence a bushel. They are roughly worth per ton about half the price of maize. Beech mast is very rich in albuminoids and oil, and is a valuable food, though in the course of collecting, the pigs lose a good deal of flesh by the exercise to which they are put. A more starchy food is required to be fed with it when it is collected. The leanness of the meat from pigs fed entirely on beech mast is such as to make it necessary for more fatty foods to be fed with it. As a rule acorns and beech mast are best used when given in small quantities to young pigs.

POTATOES AND ROOTS.

Potatoes are valuable as pig food; but pork made entirely from potatoes is very fat, and wastes much in cooking. It is necessary to give them more nitrogenous food, such as whey, butter milk, peas. beans, &c., when the full benefit of all the food is obtained. In the section dealing with cooking foods the treatment of the potato is more fully discussed.

Turnips, mangels, carrots, parsnips, and similar roots are useful as pig food. For very young and fattening pigs they may be boiled, but store pigs will eat sufficient if thrown to them in the ordinary manner. Roots should be used as an adjunct to the food rather than as a whole diet. All kinds are better for being well ripened, and if they have been pitted for some time they are improved. Pigs are kept in a healthier condition when they receive roots, especially at such time as there is no other green food available. They are the natural food for pigs, and as the pigs are fed on more concentrated food when confined than they obtain when running wild, it is the more important that they get a small share. Where pigs are fattening, they may be pulped, as less time is occupied in eating them so than when given whole. We believe breeding sows which get no other food are benefited by having a few given them; but as is explained in the section on the in-pig sow, it is absurd to make them the sole food. Cabbages of all kinds are useful and very nutritious pig food; in fact, anything of the sort that can be spared from the garden or farm, or any green stuff which would otherwise be wasted, may be profitably utilised by the pig.

Clover and Leguminous Crops.

Clover, tares, lucerne, sainfoin, and any succulent leguminous plants are highly valuable as pig food. Sufficient of these are not given to pigs. There is a great quantity of this class of crop wasted, which if given to the pigs might be turned to good account. In England these crops are almost sacred to the horse, bullock, and sheep, and few pig keepers seem to recognise how thoroughly well adapted they are to the production of pork. Whether the pigs are penned on the crop, or the green food is brought to the pigs, matters little, though in very hot or very cold weather the pigs require to be in the shade ; and in wet weather they trample more into the ground than is profitable. Grass is also an important pig food. Breeding sows never do better and never throw stronger or better litters than when they get the run of a grass field. The roadside sow produces the best litter, because she is living a natural life ; she may be too finely bred, or may have been pampered, but when allowed a good run she is brought to a natural state of existence, and her breeding functions are more vigorous. Wherever practicable a piece of grass or a patch of some leguminous crop should be obtained.

Stubbles.

Corn stubbles are useful as pig runs. Not only

are the pigs benefited by the food, but a great many weeds are prevented from seeding. Wherever that pest hogweed (*Polyginum aviculare*) is common, pigs do special good, as they eat it voraciously. They are practically the only animals that will eat it, and they thrive on it. As this is one of the most objectionable weeds on arable land, particularly on light soils, it is well that something should destroy it and prevent its seeding. When pigs are turned out, whether on grass or stubbles, they should have a ring placed in their snouts to prevent them grubbing up the earth.

Dairy Refuse.

Whey and butter-milk are the chief refuses from the dairy, and are turned to excellent account by pigs. It is recognised that one of the profits of dairying must come from the pigs, in fact they are a necessary adjunct of the dairy. It is generally calculated that where cheesemaking is practised a pig should be raised on the whey of each pair of cows, though, of course, the quantity must be regulated by the other feeding ; but if it gets a run on grass and is allowed to pick about generally, a pig can be run on each pair of cows, without other food until it is put up to fatten off. The whey may then be mixed with meal, when meat of best quality will be produced. Butter-milk is equally valuable. Both should be allowed to become sour before being consumed. The wash-tub should be a stock-pot into which any clean refuse from the dairy or house may be thrown, and many farmers keep a second tub into which the meal is put to soak for a few days previously to being consumed. This is a good practice. Fresh skim milk is apt to produce indigestion and acidity, but these rarely occur when the milk or whey has been allowed to sour naturally.

BREWERS' GRAINS.

Brewers' grains are valuable as pig food, especially for sows when suckling, as they excite the flow of milk. The feeding value of grains is not great, but they make a very good mixture with starchy foods. Modern brewery machinery is now so complete that almost all the starchy matter is extracted, but the quantity of starchy matter left in the grains is partly dependent on the thoroughness with which the barley is malted. Thoroughly malted barley leaves little starchy matter which will not be extracted during the process of malting, but evenly malted barley leaves much that cannot be converted into wort. Grains obtained from small breweries, where the machinery is not of the best class, are more valuable than those from the best fitted breweries. Grains may be stored for a long time without being injured, provided they are tightly compressed and air is prevented from entering. The grains are practically converted into ensilage. It is therefore advisable to purchase them in summer when the demand is light, and the price low, and store them for winter use. The cheapness of other feeding stuffs renders grains proportionately less valuable than they used to be, but as they are in strong demand for dairy cows the price has not fallen relatively in most places.

COAL AND CINDERS.

Coal and cinders can scarcely be ranked as foods, but they are necessary for pigs in confinement, as without them their digestive organs fail to make best use of other foods supplied, the stomach gets out of order, acidity develops, and the whole system is deranged. Whatever is withheld, coal or cinders must be given; failing these—they are practically always obtainable—a spadeful or two of fresh earth should be placed in the sty. This will be eaten and will neutralise acidity. When running loose pigs get a corrective as they require, but when shut up in yards they get only what is given them.

SECTION V.

BREEDING.

The Season and Age to Breed.

Spring is essentially the season for breeding. All animals naturally bring forth their young at this season, as the weather is becoming warmer, and the supply of food is greatest in summer, when the young have to begin to forage for themselves. Although when in domestication pigs are not dependent on the food which is raised at any particular time, there is no doubt that pigs farrowed early in the year thrive better than those born later. A pig born in November rarely thrives unless it is very warmly housed, and those a month or two earlier are not sufficiently strong to run in the open yards during winter unless the season is particularly mild. However, as the sow breeds more than twice in a year, it is impossible to restrict the breeding to the spring, but when arranging for a yilt or maiden sow to breed, it ought to be put to the boar at such a time that the young are born in January or February. The best trade for little pigs is always met with in February, March, and April, as when the days lengthen the little pigs grow most, and this is understood by all experienced pig keepers.

The season at which to put the boar to the sow to bring forth young in January is September or October, as the period of gestation, or time that the sow carries her young, is sixteen weeks. In selecting a yilt for breeding one should be chosen that was born early in the year. A sow should bring forth her first litter when she is twelve months old, she would therefore go to the boar at eight months. A yilt born late in the year would not be old enough for breeding in January or February. Yilts take the boar at a much younger age if permitted to, but it is more profitable not to let them breed when too young.

When the sow brings forth a litter in January or February she will in ordinary course produce another litter in June or July, a season when food is plentiful and the weather warm. Small pigs are little liable to cramp and chills when born at this season, and they become strong before winter. A sow pigging at the two seasons mentioned is more profitable than one breeding at intermediate periods. The first litter produce small pork suitable for eating in hot weather, when coarse pork is considered heavy and unpalatable. It is also ready to meet the early autumn pork trade—the pork season popularly being reckoned from September to May. A pig born in January is eight months old in September. It is reckoned that with ordinary good doing, a pig should produce a score of meat each month; thus, a January pig should weigh eight scores in September, and eight scores is looked upon as the typical weight of a porker, as it possesses reasonable size without undue grossness. Of course pigs can be made to grow to greater weights when fed at high pressure as for shows, but the farmer is following a rational and sound course when he aims at a score per month.

THE MANAGEMENT OF IN-PIG SOWS.

There is rarely any difficulty in getting the yilt to come into season. If she does not it is generally because her food is of too cooling a nature, such as thin wash, roots, or other green food, which should be changed for something more heating. Barley brings the yilt or sow into season most quickly, but wheat, peas, beans, or maize soon accomplish it. A yilt should not be too fat, as it will probably produce a small litter, and there is danger at the time of farrowing if she is overfat. There is greater danger of difficulty at farrowing in the case of an overfat sow than in that of a very fat yilt.

The sow need cost very little to keep during the earlier portion of the time that she is in pig, in fact they are generally better for being kept in low ·condition, though they should not be kept so low as to become weak. Exercise almost up to the time of farrowing is highly beneficial, and there are less chances of difficulty when pigging than if kept ·closely confined. Where available there is nothing better than a grass run, as a sow will support herself on grass, and a little help from the wash tub. However, during the last few weeks, which is the time when the greatest tax is made on her system—for it is then that the young pigs make nearly all the growth—the sow should receive help. Overfeeding should be guarded against, as she is liable to become too fat, especially when fed on starchy foods. What she requires is something that will help to build up the frame of the young within her. A diet of starchy foods only does not supply her with proper materials, and unless she gets something else an undue strain is thrown upon her, so that the young ones are weakly or she becomes so weak that she cannot produce them, while nature sometimes revolts and the young are expelled before the proper time. The sow does not require an entirely fattening diet, but one which will form muscle and bone also.

Foods containing nitrogen are necessary, for these supply what is needed. Feeding stuffs containing nitrogen are especially valuable, as they almost always contain lime, potash, and other constituents necessary for the building up of the frame. Turnips and mangels are often objected to, because they are said to bring about too early parturition. If the diet consists of these and nothing but other weak starchy foods, this does occur sometimes, for the reasons previously given, but the cause is a negative rather than a positive one. Roots contain little besides starch and water, and little pigs cannot be made of these—other additional food is required. A few roots are decidedly beneficial where grass or other green food is not obtainable, as they help to keep the animal healthy, but they should not form the chief portion of the diet of an in-pig sow. If fed rationally, and she is allowed a fair amount of exercise, she will rarely give much trouble at parturition. When kept in the farm yard, freshly-cut clover, grass, tares, or cabbages should be supplied, and these, with the pickings she gets in the yard, will generally suffice her, as they all contain a fair amount of nitrogen. Water, or, better, whey or skim milk must be supplied.

Down-pigging Sows.

Sows are said to be down-pigging when they nearly approach the period of farrowing. It is important that they are not hunted by other animals, and it is generally advisable to house them at night when they are gone with young for fourteen or fifteen weeks. If they are placed in the sty where they are to farrow they get accustomed to it, and are generally more tractable at the time of pigging. When put in a strange place only a short time previously, they are often very uneasy both before and immediately after pigging. A limited amount of litter should be supplied, and this should be short. The cavings made during threshing corn are the best for the purpose. If the straw is long the young are liable to become entangled in it, and if it is given in too large quantity they are often buried, and the sow lies on them and kills them. The bed should be kept small for a few days after farrowing, as weakly pigs cannot move over a thick bed, and die because of want of food or from cold. The danger at the time of farrowing is lessened if the sow's bowels are kept open for a few days preceding it. The act of parturition is rendered more easy, and there is less fear of milk fever. A small quantity of Epsom salts placed in the wash which is given her about a week before her time is up, and again about two days before farrowing, will effect all that is necessary. If by chance a sow drops her young considerably sooner than she should in the course of nature, the young, the birth bed, and the litter should be destroyed by burning, as slipping is not unfrequently the result of a contagious affection caused by a specific germ. The sty should be disinfected with chloride of lime or other disinfectant.

PARTURITION.

When the sow is about to bring forth in proper course, she shows signs of it by carrying about straw in her mouth to make a nest; the udder becomes distended, and the parts behind increase in size. These symptoms are frequently noticeable some days before actual parturition, while in other cases they precede it by only a short time. When once these signs are apparent, it is evident that her time is approaching, and she should be kept under observation. Sows rarely require assistance if they have been kept rationally fed and exercised, in fact it is difficult to give aid; but it is advisable for some one to be in attendance to help the young ones, or they are liable to be suffocated or chilled. In case the womb becomes protruded or inverted, it should be replaced as soon as possible, and if it has become affected by dirt or dung it should be washed with slightly warmed water previously. A stitch or two may be required to keep it in its place, and these should be placed through the lips of the orifice. An easy method is to pass a tight ligature round the protruded parts, when in the course of a few days they will slough off.

As the young ones are born it is advisable to take them away and place them in a warm place until the last is born, particularly if they come slowly. It is customary to wipe them with a cloth, as they are less likely to be chilled. This will prevent the sow from lying on them or otherwise injuring them in her struggles. If the sow is quite quiet there is less need for it, but it is a wise precaution. The next step is to take away the after-birth, as the sow has a tendency to eat it. This is dangerous, because it is likely to induce her to eat the little ones, which have a similar smell to it, especially if they have not been wiped. When once a sow takes to eating her young she is incurable. As soon as the sow ceases pigging, the young ones should be laid up against her and allowed to suckle. As the front teats contain the most milk, it is well to allow the weaker ones to suckle there; if left to themselves the stronger ones will get the best teats. Should there be more pigs than can be suckled, the weakest should be destroyed. It is always advisable that the person present should be the attendant to whom the sow is accustomed. Some sows are very savage during parturition ; even those docile at other times sometimes become so, and should be treated guardedly.

BREAKING OFF TEETH OF LITTLE PIGS.

Occasionally the sharp incisor teeth of little pigs give trouble at suckling, as in their struggle for a teat the pigs make careless and sometimes angry snatches at it, which results in laceration, causing the sow to become savage. When this occurs while the pigs are very young, the sow is apt to kill them, and if she tastes blood she eats them ; this establishes her as a pig-killer, and ruins her for breeding. To prevent this some breeders snap off the teeth with a pair of nippers as soon as the pigs are born. The instances where injury arises from laceration of the teat are comparatively rare, and if the sow is watched and the state of the teats noticed, it is perhaps sufficient to remove the teeth when traces of injury are noticed. Another injury arising from sore teats is that the sow will not allow the pigs to suckle ; as soon as they seize the teats she gets up and thrusts the pigs from her. The danger of this is that the pigs do not get sufficient milk, and as the sow is not properly milked, her milk gets stale, and the little pigs are upset by it. In bad cases the udder gets out of order, and milk derangements are caused, which sometimes imperil the life of the sow. Whether the teeth are got rid of at birth or not it is an important matter to see that the sow does not suffer from them, and at the sign of any irritation they should be promptly removed.

The Sow after Parturition.

The sow does not require heavy feeding immediately after farrowing; indeed, it is better that her food should be of a slushy nature to prevent any danger of milk fever. Well-soaked bran or middlings, mixed with water, whey, or buttermilk, will suffice for a day or two, when, if she appears to be all right, she may be put on a good diet of barley meal, oat-meal, and bran. When once danger from milk fever is over she requires to be well fed, so that she may have a plentiful supply of milk for her young. This is necessary, because it is important that the little ones should thrive from the first; a check during the first few weeks, whereby the young get pot-bellied and hide-bound, leaves traces which are not easily obliterated, and renders them likely to be attacked with one of the several ailments which affect little pigs. When the sow has got back her strength she should be allowed to go out of the sty for an hour or two occasionally, but as the young suckle frequently at first, she should not be kept from them too long. If she can get a run in a grass field it is all the better. In the course of ten days or a fortnight, according to their strength, the young ones may be turned out with her if the weather is mild, but if cold and wet they are best kept under cover. Both sow and young are benefited by exercise under favourable conditions. The feeding of the sow should be done regularly and frequently, otherwise the milk is liable to become sour or otherwise prejudicial to the young. Mouldy or heated

G

meal should not be given, as this is likely to contaminate the milk. Anything which vitiates the milk should be avoided, as diarrhœa is soon set up in the young pigs. Pigs require coal or cinders to aid their digestion, and it is highly important that they are not withheld at this period, as acidity is greatly prevented by them and digestion is accelerated.

SUCKING PIGS IN HEALTH AND SICKNESS.

During the first fortnight the pigs rely on their mother for sustenance, and if she has plenty of milk they thrive better so than on mixed food. Occasionally, however, the mother has a short supply of milk, and it is necessary to supplement it artificially. Additional food must be rich and easily digested. A gruel of skim milk, oatmeal, and bran is the most suitable food on such occasions, and they should be tempted to eat it as soon as possible. Whilst with the mother it is useless to place their food in the compartment the mother occupies (except when she is away from them at exercise), as she will consume it. A partition through which the little ones can pass should be put up, and in this a small feeding trough placed. The sow's trough should be too high for them to eat out of, as her food is generally too coarse and often too stale for them to eat without injury. Warm milk is a good foundation for food for young pigs, and in this bran and barley meal may be mixed. There is a danger in giving milk to young pigs, especially when the mother's milk is rich and plentiful, particularly in the case of breeds which are liable to be very fat when young. A common ailment, often called "going off their feet," is caused by too rich food. By rich food in this case is meant food with an excess of nitrogenous matter in its composition. When pigs go off their feet they lose the power of their limbs, lie helplessly and in a semi-comatose condition, caring little for their food or surroundings. It is a partial paralysis, caused by an excess of nitrogen in the blood, which oppresses the brain. The losses from this are so frequent that it is important to guard against it by supplying them with less forcing food. If there is any sign of it the additional milk should be withdrawn, a small quantity of Epsom salts or betony (sometimes locally called madder) be mixed with the food, and foods of a starchy rather than nitrogenous nature be given. If the case is a very bad one bleeding should be resorted to, the object being to attenuate the blood.

Betony is a very serviceable herb to the pig keeper, and many pig keepers keep it constantly at hand. It has active medicinal properties which are specially effective on young pigs, though it is beneficially given to older pigs, as it rectifies most common ailments, and induces them to eat when almost all other things fail. It may be given to them freshly plucked, or the dried leaves may be powdered and mixed with the food. It has an old reputation among pig keepers, and at one time was a favourite medicine among mankind. An old Spanish proverb says, "Sell your coat and buy betony," so highly was it esteemed. Although it has lost its old position in the light of other medicinal discoveries, it is still popular among pig keepers, and we think deservedly so, as we have seen such good effects from its use on many occasions.

When pigs have shown signs of going off their feet the return to milk should be made cautiously, and it should be mixed with a plentiful quantity of water.

With reasonable precautions against a too nitrogenous diet, little pigs may be gradually brought to eat almost any food by the time they are fit to leave the sow. It is highly important, however, that only small quantities, such as they will clear up at one feeding, are given. If the food stands in the trough it becomes stale. The trough, too, should be well scraped out each time. Any food of a stale or mouldy nature is dangerous whilst their stomachs are young and weak.

As is natural, young pigs require the warmest housing. They are very subject to chills; no small proportion succumb to cold, while many others are temporarily or permanently injured so far as to be profitless. It is not only necessary to procure a warm sty, but the floor should be warm also. A cold wet floor is fatal to their thriving. A damp bed, whether from natural moisture or from moist litter, is the cause of most of the ailments to which little pigs are subject. For a few days after the sow pigs it is advisable not to disturb the bed, as by doing so the sow is apt to be made uneasy, but in the course of three or four days it may be removed; after which a fresh supply should be given daily, the stale litter being removed previously. The sow recognises the advantage of a good dry bed, for if she is housed under unfavourable circumstances she always makes her nest on a dry spot, and never willingly allows it to become foul. Fœtid smells about the sty are prejudicial. The litter should be short, and by preference wheat straw should be used.

The Sucking pig is generally looked upon as a delicacy. The little roaster is particularly sweet and delicate in flavour. Charles Lamb immortalised the dish in an essay on its virtues. It is probable he wrote it while anticipating the pleasure of eating it rather than afterwards, for by some it is found rather too rich. It, however, cannot be denied it is both a popular and savoury dish. It was a little hard that Lamb should have said of the sucking pig just roasted that "ten to one he would have proved a glutton, a sloven, an obstinate, disagreeable animal, wallowing in all filthy conversation," for the pig is very much what he is made to be, and is naturally not by any means the dirty sloven he is forced to be; but, he adds, from these sins he is happily snatched away,

> " Ere sin could blight or sorrow fade
> Death came with timely care."

The sucking pig should be as plump as possible, and death's timely aid should reach him when from three to four weeks old, as after that he begins to lose some of the sweetness and delicacy associated with the roaster. The smaller breeds, which are particularly plump, make the best roasters. The roaster should be entirely milk-fed. It should be stuck, and all the blood be allowed to drain out of it.

CASTRATION.

The last step before weaning is to castrate the boar pigs, and to spay the females in those cases where they are not required for breeding. We once read an essay on the breeding and management of rams, where the writer stated that they should be castrated when a fortnight old—a mistake which could not be corrected in practice. Before castrating any of a litter, those which are to be left for breeding should be decided upon. It is generally advisable to allow an experienced operator to perform, not so much on account of the boars as the yilts. Castration is a very simple process, and when effected on young pigs injures them very slightly, even temporarily. It is a common practice among some of the pig dealers who buy young pigs to be sold at a distance to castrate them and put them at once into a hamper to travel a long journey. The spaying of the sow pigs is a matter of more skill, as an incision has to be made in the flank and the ovaries extracted, involving a surgical operation demanding experience. When yilts are not spayed they are called open yilts or sows, according to age. A spayed yilt fattens better than one unspayed, as when unspayed she becomes restless on each occasion of coming into season. Before she comes under the influence of seasons, about her fourth or fifth month, she grows rather more quickly than one spayed; for this reason it is not an uncommon thing for unscrupulous dealers to make an incision but nothing more. As the purchaser has no other guide to go by he is often deceived.

If castration and spaying are effected before the pigs are taken from the sow, any little check they might get is lessened, because they still have their mother's milk to nourish them. If done afterwards, when first put on to less nutritious foods they naturally are not so well fitted to withstand the shock.

Castration and spaying are sometimes carried out on animals of greater age, even after breeding. There is then greater risk, as the shock to the system is much more severe. Boars sometimes become so wild that it is dangerous to leave them uncut. An old boar is not very valuable as meat, as the flesh is rank, hard, and coarse. Before castration, at whatever age, the pigs should be fasted for a day; this is especially necessary in the case of the sow pigs. A moderate amount of food only should be given on the day of castration; suckling is all that is advisable. Ruptured pigs are best got rid of as soon as possible.

WEANING.

Little pigs are taken from their mother when from six to eight weeks old. Unless they are very strong and have learnt to eat freely, great care has to be exercised at six weeks, as they are very liable to be stunted, which entails a loss far heavier than any gain made by taking them from the sow when so young. The advantage of taking them from the sow at the earlier age is that she comes into season more quickly. The sow rarely comes into season when being suckled, though she does so occasionally, therefore there is an inducement to get the pigs away from her early. The gain is that of a fortnight's food saved to the sow, the loss a check on the growth of the pigs. Taking one time with another it is better to sacrifice the sow's keep. If, however, she has a small litter of strong pigs, it is sometimes more profitable to let her go to the boar early. After producing and bringing up a big litter she has undergone a strong physical strain, and she will probably throw a stronger litter next time for having a longer rest. If she produces only three or four pigs the effort has been a slight one, and she may reasonably be put to the boar in a short time. Broadly speaking, if she has produced a large litter the young should be left with her for eight weeks. But as the litter is smaller they may be taken from her sooner. If a sow throws but three or four pigs, and another sow pigging at about the same time also produces a small litter, the two litters may be put together, leaving one of the sows free to be put to the boar earlier.

For a few days previously to weaning the supply of food to the sow should be curtailed, so as to check the flow of milk, and as soon as the young are taken from her she should be given two ounces of Epsom salts, for the same reason, especially in those cases where the young are taken from her early. The weaning should be a gradual process, the pigs being kept from her for several hours at a time, which

will induce them to turn to the trough for food. If
gradually restricted they will not feel the loss of
milk so severely, and the sow will lose her milk
without inconvenience. It is important that the sow
does not get inflammation of the udder or teat. If
there are signs of it she should be relieved of a
portion of her milk. The udder should be bathed
with warm water and rubbed with grease, which
will keep the skin pliable and keep out the cold.

The Sow at Weaning.

The future of the sow should have been decided
previously to weaning. It is a mistake to discard a
sow on her first litter unless she has glaring faults,
such as a great lack of milk, milk fever, savageness
so far as destroying her young, inversion of the
uterus, or expulsion of the rectum. A small litter, or
a somewhat deficient supply of milk, and uneveness
in the size of the pigs, are not uncommon at the
first time of breeding, but may be corrected subsequently; carelessness, which results in the sow lying
on her young and suffocating them, is sometimes
due to temporary weakness or over-fatness, which
may be rectified. If, however, on the second breeding she does not improve she is best got rid of. If
a purchased sow, which has bred before, turns out
badly on her first breeding, she should be parted
with without hesitation, as the odds are that she
has been sold for faults or vice.

SECTION VI.

MANAGEMENT OF PIGS.

FEEDING YOUNG PIGS.

The little pig has been discussed up to the point where it leaves its mother, and has to be kept without regard to her. The weaning accomplished, it is important to feed the pig carefully, because the mother's milk acts as a corrective to, or at any rate aids the digestion of, other food given with it. The young pig's food should be simple, sweet, fairly rich, plentiful, and frequently given. On many farms pigs are bred but not kept after they leave the sow, while on others none are bred but many are fed.

The cottager, allotment holder, or in fact all who keep a small number of pigs are specially interested in the pig at this age : they are either buyers or sellers, generally buyers.

The future of the pig must be decided upon before it leaves its mother, and its feeding must be much in accordance with the object in view. It may be intended that it shall be fattened right away without a check, or it may be run as store before being put up to fatten. Whatever the object, it is a great gain if there is a supply of milk available; the loss of the mother's milk is then less severely felt, and no check takes place. Bran, with a little barley meal stirred into the milk, and a little whole wheat or oats occasionally thrown to the pigs, will keep them going on well for the first few weeks, when, as they get stronger, they may be given a little pea meal in mixture with the rest of the food. It is well to let milk, bran or pollards, and barley meal form the basis of food for young pigs; though often the farmer will have at command other foods in the place of those mentioned. When milk cannot be obtained, water must be used to form the slushy food they require, and fine pollard or finely-ground oats should be added. In fact the food should be somewhat regulated by the relative cost of the different feeding stuffs. It is not absolutely necessary (though it is preferable) that milk and barley meal be given, provided the food is carefully prepared, the sty is kept clean and sweet, and the pigs are fed frequently. Food which is decidedly heating should be avoided. Such a mixture as wheat meal and pea meal would certainly be a trying one to very small pigs, though they do well on milk, wheat meal, and maize meal. The characteristics of different feeding stuffs are treated with in the section on "Foods," and according to the stocks available a suitable diet may be arranged. When the object is to hurry out the pig quickly, or to keep it in show condition, milk, barley meal, and pollards are almost necessaries.

REARING LITTLE PIGS.

Cleanliness and warmth are of almost more im-

portance than is food. The best food is of little
avail if the sty is cold or dirty. Cold and dirt often
go together, as a dirty sty affords a cold bed. Pigs
require clean bedding, as those which lie on wet
dungy straw are almost certain to get chills, which
either affect the lungs or give rise to rheumatism and
cramp, with various other ailments, such as sty-
bake. The food must be given in an injudicious
manner if young pigs get very unhealthy when the
sty is kept clean, well ventilated, and warm.

As a guide to those who have not had great
experience with pigs, the following notes should be
useful. Very little experience is required to tell if a
young pig is healthy. The skin of a healthy pig is
clear and bright, the eye is bright, and even when
fat there is something perky about it. When out of
health the eye is dull, there is frequently a hacking
cough, the animal looks thin in the flank, and generally listless. No animal shows more quickly when
it is out of order. A pot-belly is a sign that the
pig has been badly managed at some time, and the
purchaser should look keenly for signs of health. If
pot-belliedness is accompanied with a dirty, harsh,
hide-bound skin, commonly called sty-baked, do not
hesitate about buying it—make up your mind to
leave the pig alone, at any price. Pigs may be lean
and dirty, but perfectly healthy, only waiting for
better opportunities to thrive; these are good pigs
to buy, but let them not be confounded with the sty-
baked pig.

To those who have not experience in animals it is
difficult to explain what indicates thriftiness in the

appearance of a pig. It is very easy to see it when it is there. When buying pigs, a thrifty pig is the one to purchase. To those of little experience it is, perhaps, most easily explained by making a comparison between a boy and a young pig. It is almost always possible to guess which of two boys of similar size will grow to be the bigger man; there is a general suggestion of sappiness and power of development in one that the other does not possess. The same holds good in the case of the pig. It is the outcome of breeding. Now as to the outcome of feeding and proper home management. Take two boys of the same age—one brought up on proper lines, the other a gutter child, lean, pasty-faced, old in appearance, skin drawn tight, stunted. The man to which he will grow will differ very little from him: the poor boy is sty-baked, and will no more make a healthy, strong, well-set-up man than will the sty-baked pig become healthy and thriving. The other boy—free of limb, healthy in skin, and open in countenance—will become a strong man.

When buying a pig, look for the one that is to suit your purpose. If it is to become a strong store, ultimately to be made up to a heavy-weight, look for one with long body, deep between the shoulders and flank, thick in the loin, broad in the back, not too pug-faced, broad between the ears, shoulders and legs set on square; all combined with health, sappiness, and good walking powers. Avoid a long, thin, narrow head, a sunk back, coarse ears and tail, narrow ribs and thin flank, rupture, narrow fore-quarter, and gauntness as opposed to sappiness. If a pig is required to come to quick maturity it may be more cobby in build, rather shorter and thicker proportionately, with shorter head; all parts should show roundness, as indicating quick fattening powers; the bone should be fine.

CLEANLINESS OF STIES.

The previous remarks (explaining desirable and undesirable features in the pig at the time it is weaned) are applicable to store pigs of all ages. The management of pigs can now be further discussed. Pigs should not be allowed to lie on hot or wet dung, but the danger is greatest when pigs are young, for they are then most liable to contract ailments. The bed should be made of sweet litter, supplied daily. The straw which has been used as bedding may be utilised to cover the remainder of the sty, to absorb urine and keep the pigs from direct contact with the cold floor. If carefully bedded, the pigs will do their share towards keeping it clean. No animal takes so much trouble to keep its droppings away from its bedding; it almost always selects one corner for this purpose. These should be shovelled out daily. Where space is limited, a little burnt earth scattered where the droppings have been thickest acts as the best disinfectant, besides absorbing moisture and preventing it spreading to other parts of the sty. At least once a week the sty should be entirely cleaned and the floor washed down, but the pigs should not be allowed to return until it is dry.

BEDDING.

Wheat straw is the best litter for pig sties. It lasts longest and tends to keep the pigs clean and free from lice. Barley straw always tends to make pigs lousy, they then get uncomfortable, restless, and do not thrive. Oat straw is better than barley, but less good than wheat. Saw-dust is a healthy form of bedding, as are also wood shavings, though the latter are not good absorbents of manure. Good peat moss free from earthy matter is also healthy. Whenever these short litters are used the droppings should be removed frequently, and occasionally the litter should be thrown up into heaps to allow the floor to sweeten. Straw is best where obtainable, because it makes the best manure. Litter used in the sty may be turned into the court to be trodden into manure. If the floor is provided with a raised wooden bench or slatted floor, a very small quantity of straw is sufficient to make a bed, though in cold sties during very severe weather the bedding should be plentiful, so that the pigs may curl up in it. It is always economical to shake up that portion of the straw which is not thrown out of the sty daily. Let it not be forgotten that foul sties mean unhealthy pigs, and if this is acted upon there will be comparatively few diseases.

PORKERS.

The feeding of young pigs to be sold as porkers, at from three to five scores, should be done on the foods mentioned. The quantity must be regulated by the quantity they will eat and by the apparent health. It is difficult to ascribe definitely what quantity shall be given to a pig at a certain age, as there are several causes affecting the appetite even of a healthy pig. The best guide is the appetite of the animal, it may eat more or less at one time than another. The best course to take is to give just as much as the pig will clear up at each meal. If any is left in the trough it is a proof that too much is given, and this often causes pigs to become dainty. It is as a rule best to keep to one general food, but a little green stuff of one kind or another may be given with advantage.

If pigs scour it is a proof that something is wrong with them, and it is generally attributable to cold or to unsuitable feeding. The pigs may be over-fed, eating more than they can properly digest; the food may be stale or too strong for them. Scour is often contagious, consequently it is highly important to keep the sties clear of it in the first instance. The quantity of meal in the wash requires increasing gradually as the pigs are able to take it; if the food is rapidly increased in strength scour is likely to be set up, and instead of doing good will cause a check, rendering the feeding for four or five days useless. It is a principle in the feeding of all animals that the food should be increased gradually and moderately, and the nearer animals are to consuming as much as their system will assimilate the greater is the necessity for care.

FEEDING HEAVY PIGS.

The pigs which are to be kept to produce heavy pork require good feeding when taken from their mother; they are better for good feeding at all times, but it is not necessary to feed them at high pressure from start to finish. They should never be allowed to run down in condition so as to get stunted. Because a pig is not fat at a given time it is not necessarily stunted, it may be lean and thriving. Pigs of large breeds have a tendency to make frame rather than to lay on fat when young, and if they are to be grown to a heavy size their time is not wasted in doing so, as the fat can be laid on cheaply afterwards. Where the pig keeper buys the whole of his food, and this is of a concentrated nature, it is advisable to keep the animals on the fat side, as less time and less food are required to bring the animal to maturity. When, however, the food is of a coarse nature, such as is frequently met with on the farm, the pigs consuming this need not necessarily be kept really fat; they should, however, be better pigs and more valuable day by day. Strong stores consuming coarse farm waste are often as profitable as any portion of the farm stock, and in their scavenging turn to profitable account much which would go to waste. It is absurd to think that because a pig is finding part of his living he is necessarily unprofitable, though this idea prevails among some high feeders. It is equally foolish to think that a scavenging pig will be profitable if it does not get sufficient food to keep increasing in size daily. Because a pig scavenges it is no reason that it should not receive additional food, in fact all reasonable farmers do give the pigs extra food. Turning pigs into a yard in summer time to find a living among the horse droppings turned out of the stable, and giving them nothing else but water, is folly, though many pigs have gone through this experience, but not with profit to themselves or their owners. From our earliest days we, personally, found a good thriving store a profitable animal, and as our pocket money in boyhood was limited to the profit we made out of the pigs kept in the yards at one of the farms, and we managed to get some pocket money, we still have regard for stores. We then rarely kept anything but breeding sows and stores, and these were fed almost exclusively on the offal of the farm, nothing but bran being purchased. So much food would not reach the pigs, or to anything else for that matter, if they were not allowed to do a little foraging, that we are certain almost every farm can run a few stores with advantage; but they should be kept in a good growing condition, as stunted stores are slow feeders. Whether the pigs, as they increase in weight, have been fed heavily from the time they were weaned, or have passed through the store stage, they require to be fed well to bring them to the butcher. Up to eight scores weight pigs may be regarded as small pork, very suitable for consumption when fresh killed, but after that they may be considered on the large size, though up to fifteen scores they are not actually coarse, though they are more agreeable when cured at this size

than when eaten fresh. After fifteen scores the pig
is best suited for bacon, and he may be made up to
any weight the market calls for. Under most circumstances fifteen scores is as far as it is profitable
to take them; it is better then to put the food before
another lot. It must always be remembered that as
the weight increases the price per pound decreases.

It takes much to upset a strong hog; his
capacity for eating and his powers of digesting and
assimilating food are marvellous. He wants plenty,
and that good. 'It is not of greatest importance
what the food is provided it is blended into a wholesome diet; he will cope with it. He requires feeding
three times a day with stiff meal-porridge, preferably
mixed with milk, failing that water. The effect of
various feeding stuffs is given in the section on foods.
Let him clear up at each meal, and keep his sty
warm, but well ventilated, and let him be disturbed
as little as possible. Strong pigs suffer much less
from cold or foul sties than do little ones. This is
not intended as an excuse for leaving him to remain
filthy, but in large sties where several pigs are lying
they keep the dung so compressed underneath them
that there is little chance for it to heat or to throw
off objectionable or injurious fumes. Consequently
many, in fact most, feeders allow the manure to
accumulate under the pigs for a long time, and only
clear it out when absolutely necessary. The pigs
suffer very little; in fact, if the bedding is kept dry,
except from the droppings of the animals, it is
probable that pigs thrive as well like this as in any
other way. Sufficient room, however, must be given

them to make their droppings other than on the bed.
Fresh straw should be thrown in daily. The more
heavily a pig is fed, and the longer he is kept
enclosed, render it more important that coal or
cinders are daily placed before him. If the fattening
pigs rootle up their beds too much so as to disturb
the dung and cause it to heat, they should have a
ring placed through the nose.

MANAGEMENT OF THE BOAR.

The young boar until such age as he shows signs
of work may be run with the other pigs of his litter.
It is preferable that he gets a full share of exercise,
as he will develop stronger and better. It is
necessary that a boar is active, and if he gets
exercise when young it will stand him in good stead
throughout his life. In fact, at all times he is better
when he gets full opportunity for exercising, and it
is preferable if he can run into a grass paddock, as
the grass he finds there is a great source of health
to him, and he is far more likely to beget strong
and numerous litters than when kept in a confined
sty on nothing but concentrated food. If accommodation is limited and a grass run not available he
should be plentifully supplied with green food—in
summer grass, vetches, lucerne, cabbages, or similar
foods; in the winter and spring, when the foregoing
are scarce, swedes, mangels, kohl rabi, carrots and
parsnips. In autumn swedes are best, kohl rabi in
winter, carrots and parsnips in early spring, and
mangels in late spring. Swedes are at their best
before March; mangels are at their best after March.

The boar should not be used until he is at least nine months old, if used before he will not be useful to a full age. If not used until nine months, then allowed only a fair amount of work, and given rational food and exercise, he will keep serviceable until five years old. It is often recommended that he be limited to thirty sows, but it will not hurt him to take a sow a week when full grown.

By close confinement and want of proper exercise to wear them down, the boar's hoofs frequently grow to such length that he is thrown right back on to his pasterns, and can travel only with difficulty. This should be guarded against; but if allowed to get long they must be cut off. A fat heavy boar with bad feet becomes almost useless. Should the boar become savage the tusks should be sawn off, so as to render them ineffectual. When long they are exceedingly dangerous and inflict bad wounds. The village blacksmith will take off the teeth.

An old boar has not much value as meat, but if castrated he will pay for the feeding. The skin is very thick, and the flesh strong, tough, and of poor quality. A fat boar is an animal to sell rather than to eat at home. He is most usefully disposed of when sold for bacon purposes. A cut boar is called a stag. The meat is best when newly laid on, therefore it is as well to let the boar be low in condition at the time of castration, to let him run out and be fed on green foods for a time, and then be fattened off quickly. The meat is then more tender and sweeter.

SECTION VII.

THE COTTAGER'S PIG.

SOURCES OF FOOD.

In the earlier sections special mention has frequently been made as to the treatment of the pig of the cottager and the amateur as well as of the farmer, but some points which particularly affect its management where kept singly or only in small quantities are worth mentioning. The pig of the garden rather than of the farm is the one alluded to here, and may be kept by the labouring man or the more wealthy householder. Its object is to consume the waste from the garden and from the house, and turn to profitable account that which otherwise would be valueless. As a rule the food from the two sources mentioned are not sufficient to fatten the animal, and some extra food, generally bran or meal, has to be provided. The feeding properties of different feeding stuffs available as pig food have been given previously, so there is no need to enter into the details again. The cottager has refuse from his house, which may be little, but that little should be used. His garden will pro-vide a good quantity of stuff which may go to the pig trough after he has taken out what he cares to use for himself and family, and if he has an allotment it is easy to provide practically all required to fatten the pig. In addition to this he can generally get grass and other green food from road sides, fences, and waste places in general. In harvest time his children can glean from the farmers' fields a very considerable quantity of grain. Later on they can collect acorns and beech mast in most districts. Living in the country all foods he purchases come at first cost; while the dung made goes to enrich the garden or allotment, so his position is in all ways most favourable.

THE STY.

His sty, if not provided by the landlord, need not be an expensive building. A warm corner of the garden should be chosen. The material may be that which is least expensive in the district. The destruction of any wooden building in the locality may provide him with all he wants, except covering for the roof. Furze closely packed between supports makes a warm sty. Rough wood from the sawyer's yard or many other inexpensive materials put up by his own hands makes the sty a cheap building to erect. A more substantial building made of old railway sleepers, stone where stone is plentiful, or bricks in those cases where expense is not a matter for serious consideration can be made to form neat, tidy, and comfortable sties.

The bottom or flooring of the sty is often rather more difficult to get, but there is in most districts something suitable near at hand. In chalk districts a good floor can be made of chalk, well rammed down and level. Gravel and lime will make a strong grout, and form a hard floor. In clay districts clay may be burned. In fact, with a little ingenuity the labourer need not be at a great expense. The roof of an outhouse of this kind can be covered and made to look tidy by thatch, which is the best and most healthy of all roofing. Wheat straws, reeds, heather, or any similar material are well adapted for thatching. Other materials mentioned in the section relating to sties may be used if preferred.

ARRANGING FOOD.

Where one pig only is kept at a time it is advisable to buy in a young one in spring. Food is then scarcest. A strong pig from an early litter is preferable. In spring the supply of food from the garden is small; in autumn it is more plentiful, consequently in autumn a strong pig can be kept with most advantage. A young pig in autumn may not clear up all the food which is available. If the young pig is bought in spring and kept in a thriving condition through summer, it can be fattened off in autumn or winter at a good weight in accordance with the supply of food at hand. The meat is then available for the labourer and his family at a time when his wages are usually not so high as in summer. A young pig from the sow eight weeks old is generally purchasable at from 12s. to 16s., but occasionally they may be bought for 8s., while sometimes when the trade is very keen they may cost 20s. Pigs of six weeks old are very often sold as eight weeks, and if very well grown pigs eight weeks old are sometimes sold as twelve weeks old. Those unaccustomed to pig purchasing should therefore be careful to deal with those whom they can trust. Well fed the pig will weigh eight scores (160 lbs.) when eight months old. At sixpence per pound this amounts to £4. There is, however, a great difference between a pig well fed and one which is kept on bare sustenance.

PROVIDING FOOD IN GARDENS AND ALLOTMENTS.

From the questions which appear in the query columns of agricultural papers it is evident that the means of providing food for pigs, although those seeking imformation have land available for the purpose, is often a difficulty ; a few hints may therefore be useful. As a rule a portion of the garden is required for producing vegetables for culinary purposes, and only a small portion is set apart for the pig. With few exceptions the vegetables required by the family are such as are well suited for pig feeding. It is a striking feature in almost all gardens that the beds of cabbages and other vegetables are generally made so large that only a small portion of the crop is consumed in the house, while the rest is wasted or fed to pigs. In gardens it is better for those with a small quantity of ground to grow nothing but vegetables suitable for house consumption, for though the more distant allotment would produce them equally well, it is more convenient to have those vegetables required daily close at hand.

It is not advisable to grow potatoes for pig consumption only, as there are always small or diseased ones which are available for the pig. Early potatoes intended for digging in July should have winter greens planted between the rows a few weeks before they are fit to dig. The greens, savoys, or Brussels sprouts then become established early and make a full crop, which they would not if the planting were postponed too long. Kale suitable for consumption in the following spring may also be planted then ; this will then be off the ground in time to be sown with a spring crop. Planted later it is of little use in early spring, as it will not have thrown side shoots. Drumhead cabbages are the most weighty cabbages, but they hold the ground a long time. They should be planted in early spring from seedbeds sown in the second week of the previous August. They are fit for feeding from September to Christmas. Early cabbages of the Imperial and Early York type may be planted out in October and November, or February. They then come in in July, and with later plantings last till September. Seedbeds from which cabbage plants are transplanted in the autumn and early spring should be sown in August. Those from which it is desired to transplant in summer should be sown at the end of March and the beginning of April.

MANGELS

should be sown in April or beginning of May. In small plots it is wisest to dibble in the seed at the required distance, about two feet from row to row,

and a foot from plant to plant in the rows. Very
little seed is then required, and there is little trouble
in cleaning. Seed requires drilling at the rate of
from six to eight pounds per acre, as a large proportion of the seed is wasted, because the plants are
destroyed in thinning. They should be stored in
October and November, and not consumed before the
New Year, better still if left until April or even June.

SWEDE TURNIPS

require seeding from May to July, and feeding from
November to March. Three pounds of seed are
required when drilled; but a quarter of an ounce is
ample per pole in a garden. White and yellow
turnips may be sown from May to August. The
quickly maturing kinds, such as the Stratton Green,
come to a good growth in from six weeks to two
months, and are specially valuable as catch crops in
gardens. They are not such good keepers as the
swede, and require eating fairly soon after maturing.

PARSNIPS

should be sown in February or March, in a fine tilth.
From six to eight pounds of seed per acre is the
usual seeding; this amounts to rather over half an
ounce on a pole of ground. With the great care
given to small plots half an ounce is sufficient. They
may be left in the ground until the ground is
required for preparation for another crop. They are
best fed in the spring.

CARROTS

should be sown from February to April. For bulk
early seeding is preferable, about the same weight

per acre or pole as recommended for parsnip seeding —a little more rather than less. Dig before frost. Suitable for winter feeding.

LUCERNE,

if kept clear of weeds, will grow more valuable green stuff than will any other plant. Drill the seed in straight rows about a foot apart, at the rate of twenty to twenty-eight pounds per acre. This is roughly two to two and a half ounces per pole. The crop will keep remunerative for several years if kept free from weeds and well manured.

SAINFOIN

is valuable, as where lime is abundant in the soil it will keep down for several years. It may be sown broadcast. Half a hundred-weight of shelled seed is required per acre; this is about five ounces per pole. Lucerne and sainfoin should be sown in April or May.

RED CLOVER

will remain profitable for two or three years on most soils. It gives little growth in the year in which it is sown, a remark which applies to all clovers; it is therefore best sown down in a corn crop. From ten to fourteen pounds per acre, or an ounce or slightly more per pole, is required. A peck of rye grass seeded with it is an advantage to the crop.

COW GRASS

is more perennial, but crops less than red clover. All clovers make good green meat for pigs, but the red or broad is most productive, and best worth growing.

VETCHES

or tares are exceedingly useful as pig feed. Green
food may be obtained from May to October from
consecutive sowings. The autumn sown vetches
are fit to feed earliest. These should be sown
in August or September, the earlier the better;
the variety for sowing at this season is the winter
vetch. Spring seeding may commence as soon as
the land can be got in order, and seeding may continue to May. Spring vetches are needed for this
season. From ten to fourteen pecks of seed are
required to sow an acre, or from four to five and a
half pounds per pole.

CORN CROPS

to provide straw for litter should be sown in
spring or autumn, according to the kind. Wheat
is best sown in October; barley and oats in
February or March. Wheat requires sowing at the
rate of from five pecks in September, when everything is favourable for its growth, to twelve pecks
late in November. Barley, eight to twelve pecks
per acre. Oats, ten to sixteen pecks.

FIELD PEAS

should be sown early in spring—February or beginning of March. Seeding, eight to ten pecks per acre.

WINTER BEANS

require seeding in September or October; spring
beans in January or February. From eight to
twelve pecks per acre required.

SECTION VIII.

AILMENTS.

SWINE FEVER AND OTHER CONTAGIOUS AILMENTS.

The pig is liable to many ailments. The great changes brought about through feeding and domestication have been done at the expense of his powers of resisting disease. No indigenous animal is so liable to chills, rheumatism, and other common complaints. He takes fevers almost as readily as a child, and catches almost any infectious or contagious disease affecting farm stock. Good management, however, will keep him reasonably free from ailments, as most of them arise from the want of recognition that he requires special care in the matter of feeding, housing, and exercise. Properly managed, he is a profitable animal to keep.

SWINE FEVER or hog cholera is unfortunately only too frequently met with, though whenever pigs look unwell it has become the practice to ascribe it to swine fever. This is not altogether an unwise course, as owing to the Contagious Diseases (Animals) Act of 1878, slaughtering of diseased animals is imperative, and omission to report outbreaks of the fever is visited with a fine should its presence be discovered. The local authority may order the herd to be slaughtered, for which compensation is made. The most skilful veterinary surgeon cannot say definitely that the pig is suffering from swine fever unless he makes a post-mortem examination, as outward symptoms of disease are very similar to those of diseases which are not contagious. When premises have been occupied by pigs suffering from the diseases, all pains should be taken to disinfect them, and all manure and litter should be removed beyond the reach of pigs. The disease is contagious and not infectious, so all traces should be destroyed. Great difficulty has been experienced in getting rid of the disease, because unless all pigs brought into contact are slaughtered, it is possible for the disease to be carried in one which has been infected for a lengthy period. A pig carries the disease until the last of the button-shaped formations in the intestines are voided, as these are one stage of the disease, and contain the germs which reproduce it. As the pigs have to be slaughtered, it is of little use to attempt to apply a remedy. Prevention is the chief means of combating it. A farmer's stock cannot be affected with it unless the disease is carried to it. A great point, therefore, is to breed rather than to buy-in pigs. No matter what care is exercised in purchasing in the open maket, it is impossible to be certain that the animals have not been in contact with others affected by it. Unless someone or something brings the disease, it cannot affect those which are sound. Unfortunately there are many ways in which the germs of the disease may be conveyed. The farmer himself or his men may carry it; the miller's cart going from one yard to another may bring it; cats or rats, and not improbably dung-flies, can all act as conveyers.

Rats are very probably carriers, as they frequent piggeries, or will travel a long way to get to the pig trough. In snowy weather the distance which rats will travel is plainly shown, therefore it is especially necessary to destroy them. Some causes can be prevented, while other sources of contagion are less under control, but it is important to exercise care wherever there is disease in a district.

The outward symptoms of the disease vary, but as a rule the pigs lose their appetite, become dull, and thirsty, sometimes have a hacking dry cough, and are generally feverish. As the disease advances, red spots break out on the skin, particularly on those parts, such as the thighs, ears, &c., where the skin is thinnest. The symptoms, however, are not confined to pigs suffering from swine fever; but the outbreak should be notified to the police, who will call in veterinary aid to determine whether swine fever exists. Most veterinary surgeons now can make a satisfactory post-mortem and determine whether the disease is present. This is satisfactory, as until recently many could not. We were mulcted in a £5 fine some years ago because a pig died, and we did not report it. It had not swine fever, but the veterinary said it had. He made no examination of it beyond a casual glance. We did not appeal, because an appeal was made against a decision given in the district but a short time before. The appeal was sustained, but it cost the farmer £100 to win his case, which was satisfaction dearly bought. We did not care to purchase satisfaction at the same rate. Good management in connection with housing, exercise, and food is the best means of fortifying the pig against attack.

FOOT AND MOUTH DISEASE.

Foot and mouth disease has wrought great havoc among pigs during various outbreaks. However, as the outbreaks are kept in check by prompt slaughter, there is no need to suggest other means of prevention and cure than those mentioned in connection with swine fever.

OTHER AILMENTS.

COUGHS.

Coughs, colds, and chills have as a rule the same origin—cold draughty sties or damp beds. Sometimes, however, lowness of condition, by which the pigs become anæmic, and thus unable to combat ordinary atmospheric changes, is productive of chills, which develop into more serious pulmonary complaints. Occasionally cough arises from indigestion. The cause of chills may be summed under two headings—1st, those which arise from bad management in the sty with regard to cleanliness and warmth ; and 2nd, those which arise from injudicious or improper feeding. The real cause may be arrived at with little observation. It is important, whatever the origin, that the pig is kept warm and on a clean bed. If the cold is persistent a mild purgative of 2 drachms each of Epsom salts and sulphur for small pigs, to 4 drachms each for larger pigs. Betony, or madder, acts as a corrective, and

I

a handful of leaves crushed in the hand and mixed with the food is beneficial.

MEASLES.

Measles attack young pigs. They usually scour, and their throats are often sore, preventing them from eating freely. Small blotches break out on the skin and in the mouth. The food must be soft and good, while in bad cases a gargle of water and vinegar is beneficial, but pigs are bad garglers or medicine takers, as they are apt to squeal at critical moments, and the medicine " goes the wrong way." Warmth and cleanliness are essential. The disease is contagious, and the outward signs are apparent for about eight days.

RHEUMATISM.

Rheumatism and cramp are very similar, and result from the same causes—cold and wet sties, and acidity produced by bad feeding. In the section relating to the feeding of young pigs, mention was made of pigs going off their feet, in which they lie helplessly about the sty. The pig suffering from rheumatism shows many symptons similar to this, but the pig gone off its feet appears to suffer no pain, whereas a rheumatic pig shows much pain on being touched or made to move. Warmth is necessary, and a dry lair imperative. Half a teaspoonful of bi-carbonate of potash mixed in the food daily will tend to decrease acidity ; and a tablespoonful of cod-liver oil twice a day will act beneficially. The parts affected may be rubbed with any liniment at hand. Sweet fresh food must be given.

TRICHINOSIS.

Trichinosis is fortunately rare in England, and the English pig keeper probably has to thank the stringent rules affecting contagious diseases for this, and in this way reaps a benefit not always apparent. The disease is due to the presence of the parasite, Trichina spinatis, which is chiefly found in the muscles, which it attacks and destroys. Animals affected in course of time develop millions of these minute parasites, and there is no known remedy. If by chance a pig is found containing them it should be destroyed by burning. The great danger of the disease is that the human body is found a suitable host for them, and if meat containing them is not very thoroughly cooked so as to destroy them, the parasites affect the consumer, and he soon dies. The immunity of English pork should always make it more valuable than American or Continental pork, because the disease prevails there more or less at all times.

DIARRHŒA.

Diarrhœa, or scour, is often associated with other diseases, but it may exist alone, having been caused by unsuitable food. It most often occurs in young pigs when suckling from sows which have been fed on stale foods, or are suffering from derangement of the milking organs. In this case the sow, as the primary cause, should be attended to and got back to a healthy condition as quickly as possible. Warmth is essential at all times when pigs are brought low by scouring. A teaspoonful of alum, with a little powdered ginger, and a teaspoonful of charcoal given twice a day is as effective as anything. Scour is generally contagious and the sties should be thoroughly cleansed and white-washed, while the floor should be sprinkled with lime, Condy's fluid, or other disinfectant. Coal or cinders should be supplied at all times as a preventive.

CONSTIPATION.

Constipation should be removed by simple purgatives. A hot bran mash, well prepared, and an ounce of Epsom salts will usually effect this.

VERMIN.

Most other ailments have been dealt with in previous sections of the book, but there are a few minor ailments or affections that may be treated with, such as lice, worms, and mange.

Lice are generally found where foul litter has been supplied. Barley straw is particularly liable to encourage them. A weak solution of tobacco juice or kerosene will get rid of them; as will Spratt's or Naldire's dog soaps. *Mange* is caused by parasites in the skin. The animal should be well washed with soft soap and water, and then dressed with dog soap.

Worms should be got rid of by means of one of the worm powders obtainable at any chemist's or veterinary surgeon's. There are several worms affecting the intestines of the pig, but all have the same effect of preventing the animal from thriving. The appetite is abnormal, but the pig gets thinner, and shows signs of irritation, rubbing itself frequently. Pigs when thriving rub themselves, but only occasionally. If a pig feeds well, and there appears no reason why it should not thrive. yet it does not, it is wise to assume it is troubled with worms, and to dose it to get rid of them.

MEDICATING A PIG.

Medicating a pig is somewhat difficult, as owing to its exertions, and the habit of squeaking when handled, the medicine is liable to enter the body via the windpipe instead of the gullet. To avoid this it is well—after having secured the pig—to make it sit up on its hindquarters, and then to place in its mouth the toe of an old shoe, the tip of which has been cut off. The pig will cease its squealing and commence to chew the shoe; while doing this, the medicine may be poured down slowly, and it will be swallowed safely. Milder medicines may be mixed with the food. The most simple way of catching a pig is to drop a running noose over its nose. Some dexterity is needed to do this, especially when the pig has been subjected to it previously. It is often necessary to suspend the noose from a long stick, and practically fish for it. It is always most easy when the pig is penned in close quarters.

RINGING PIGS.

Ringing pigs—that is, placing a ring or stud in the noses of pigs which are allowed to run in paddocks, or which contract the habit of " rootling " up dung—is a simple and effective process. In small pigs one small ring is sufficient, but in older pigs and boars a larger one, or even two are necessary. The ring takes several forms. Sometimes a pig-nail is used. This is a nail of very soft metal with a stud at the top; the lower end is sharpened, and is thrust through the cartilage of the nose, and then turned up with a pair of tweezers. A plain round ring is used sometimes. This is a curved piece of metal sharp at one end, and open at the other, which, on being closed with a pair of pincers, sockets so as to form a ring. The ring is held in the pincers in such a way that the ends abut, so that they pass through the cartilage as the pincers close. A double ring is used for big pigs. It is made with two sharpened pot-hooked ends; a bottom bar is then formed by turning both ends up so as to form a U. The ends are narrowed into a width which permits one end to be shoved through either side of the cartilage; after this the ends are turned in and the operation is complete. They are more simple than this explanation may, perhaps, suggest, as they are already constructed so that all the operator has to do is to shove the ends through the nose and pinch them down. If placed too far forward the ring will tear out; if too far back, so as to enter the flesh, it will be too painful.

Bleeding.

Bleeding is sometimes necessary. It is effected in various parts of the animal. In some districts part of the ear or tail is cut off, but this is crude, and injures the appearance of the pig. It is better to bleed from the ear by turning the ear back so as to expose the veins running over the inside. The veins are easily discerned if they are pressed with the finger near the base of the ear, as they then become more prominent. The blood will flow freely until the finger is removed, when it will soon cease, The palate veins are also well suited to the purpose. but rather more difficult to get at. The plate vein running along the inner side of the fore leg is a convenient and effective place. The vein will be easily discerned if a cord is tied round the leg near the shoulder, and it should be opened near to the knee.

SECTION IX.

FEATURES OF THE PIG TRADE.

IRREGULARITY OF PRICES.

The occasional purchaser of pigs is naturally not placed so favourably as is the man who is trading more frequently. The pig trade is very irregular, rising and falling week by week, according to supply and demand; the dealer, therefore, is able to sell pigs to novices at higher prices than he can to the farmer. But the greatest variation in prices occurs through the stock of pigs in the country becoming either abnormally high or low. The pendulum, as it were, swings backwards and forwards very rapidly. The stock falls low, and prices rise so much that there is an exceptional profit in pig keeping, consequently there is a rush to develop stocks; every available sow is put to breeding, with the result that in a year or two the country is so overstocked that pig keeping becomes temporarily unremunerative. The effect of this is to induce pig keepers to fatten off their sows and stop breeding. This results in the stock running low in a year or two, bringing about correspondingly high prices. This oscillation in prices is always in progress. Pig keepers do not seem to act on the precept of breeding in a low market to sell in a high one, but, as soon as prices reach a high point, all rush into breeding, buying high-priced breeding stock, with the result that by the time the young pigs from that stock are fit for sale the high prices have receded, and there is another glut. The proper time to buy or breed pigs is when they are very low in price, as the swing of the pendulum will have regulated the market so that by the time they are fit to kill the trade is at its zenith. Probably few pig keepers realise how quickly the stock of pigs may be increased, otherwise pig breeding would be carried out on more rational lines.

Rate of Increase of Pigs.

It has been calculated that if the whole of the female offspring of two sows be bred from for ten years, there will be 39,062,500 pigs living at the end of that period. It is arrived at in this way. Two sows a year old may be taken to produce two litters of 5 each litter, making 20 in all, of which it may be assumed that one-half are boars and one-half sows. This leaves 10 sows which give 10 pigs each, making 100, of which 50 are sows. In the third year there are 50 sows producing 500 young, 250 of which are sows ; in the fourth year, 2,500 are raised, of which 1,250 are sows. If this is carried out, it will be seen that at the end of ten years there are 39,062,500 male and female pigs living, or nearly a pig to each human being in the king-dom. In eleven years there would be 214,843,750 sows, and it is about time to stop calculations. During the same time there would be as many boar

pigs to turn into pork. When the pig keeper
realises this he is in a position to see how very easily
the pig stock can be raised beyond the requirements
of the market, and the falling in price should be a
guide to him to begin to get up his sow stock.

A great many young pigs are sold as being older
than they really are. Those who buy young pigs
should look to the dentition, a description of which
is given in a previous section. We know positively
that many thousands of pigs are sold yearly as being
eight weeks old, when they are only six, or at most
seven. Unless the temporary central incisors are
fully developed the pigs cannot be eight weeks old,
and the dealer has palmed on him younger pigs so
as to get an unfair price. At three months four
temporary incisors are well up, the lateral or side
pair being two-thirds or three-fourths as long as the
central pair. The amateur is so often imposed upon
that we think it highly important for him to look
to this point.

SECTION X.

PIG CALENDAR.

A summary of the practices which should be followed at different seasons is useful to the amateur pig keeper, and they cannot be more conveniently dealt with than in a monthly calendar.

THE MONTHS.

JANUARY.

This is recognised as the coldest month, consequently warm housing is of great importance. At the approach of severe frosts special attention should be given to secure the warmth of the sty and dryness of the floor. Damp litter should be removed regularly and a dry bed always be available. Little pigs thrive badly if allowed to run out in the cold yards. Only strong stores and breeding sows should be allowed out of the sties. The earliest and generally most profitable litters are due in this month. It is highly important that the little pigs are not allowed to stray from their mothers, as they rapidly catch chills. When the little pigs begin to feed, their food should be given them in a tepid condition. All pigs are better for a few roots. As no other green food is available, swedes, carrots, kohl-rabi, and cabbages are the most suitable now. It is a good season for killing, as meat keeps well in cold weather. Fast the pigs for at least twelve hours before killing.

Evening is a good time for killing, as the meat sets before morning, so that it can be cut up and dealt with then. Slaughtering in the evening is of most importance in warm weather, because it permits the meat to be dealt with sooner.

FEBRUARY.

The trade for store pigs begins to be more active, and it is a good season for selling young ones; as the pigs do well from this season onwards, it is also a good season for buying. This should be a busy season for breeders. Should the supply of green food and roots be short, brewers' grains will be very useful for promoting a flow of milk. Mangels grown on light land mature and develop their full feeding properties sooner than those grown on heavier soils, so that, whereas those grown on heavy land do not become fully developed until March or April; those from lighter soils are as well developed in February, and are therefore not wasteful to feed. The other roots recommended for January may be given. Spring tares may be sown for consumption in July and August. Carrots may be sown. Heavy pigs should be fed well with the view of getting them forward for the butcher. Cabbages from autumn sown seed beds should be transplanted.

MARCH.

Breeding and buying young pigs should continue. January pigs will require weaning and castration. Promising young sow pigs should be selected to run as breeding yelts. Sows on weaning should be closely watched so that they may be sent to the boar at the proper time. Cold March winds are prejudicial to young pigs, but if they can run out in the sun for a short time in a yard or court protected from wind they will benefit by it. Swedes begin to lose their feeding value, mangels become more valuable, vetches may still be sown. Preparation of land for mangels should be proceeded with. Kale is often ready for feeding at this season, and as it is the first of the newly grown green crops, is very valuable in keeping the animals healthy. Parsnips and carrots may be sown. Early potatoes may be planted.

APRIL.

Lucerne, grass, and clover often become big enough for grazing, and if the weather is mild afford good pasturing. Seed-beds of cabbages and kale should be sown to produce plants for transplanting in the summer months. Potato planting is general. Mangels may be sown at the end of the month. Heavy fattening pigs should be hurried out, or with the advent of warm weather in May they will be difficult to dispose of. Clover, lucerne, and saintoin should be sown. Young pigs will revel in sunshine if they are allowed to run out.

MAY.

Summer pig keeping may be said to commence this month. There is a plentiful range of crops which are suitable for feeding, and grass becomes long, affording good grazing. Cheese-making is commenced in many districts, and the whey is available. Any not required should be stored for future use; it is always better to let it become soured before using. In butter-making districts the flush of milk which generally attends the turning out of cows to grass produces a large quantity of butter-milk or skim milk. The heavy pork season ends when May comes in, and a small size is more market-able. Mangels may still be sown, and turnip-sowing may be commenced. Clover and vetches are fit for feeding.

JUNE.

Green food is abundant, tares, early cabbages, and many other crops being added to the list. Brewers' grains are generally cheap, and may be stored for winter use. Cabbages and kale may be transplanted from the spring-sown seed-beds. Store pigs and breeding sows find little in the yards at this season, and require proper feeding. Feeding meals are generally dear at this season, so it is not advis-able to have many fattening pigs in the sties. Store pigs thrive well on the ample supply of green food and dairy waste, and cost little to keep.

JULY.

Pig keeping at this season differs little from the preceding month. Second-early cabbages and spring-sown vetches should be plentiful. Pigs should be able to find shade in hot weather, and they require to have water or wash by them. If they can roll in a muddy pool they will be more comfortable, as this is practically the only means they have of defending themselves from flies and other insects which cause them pain and inconvenience.

AUGUST.

August is identified with harvest, and a fresh supply of food becomes available. Green fodder should, however, be freely used, particularly as such crops as tares, when maturing, are very rich in feeding matter. Transplanting of cabbages and winter greens may be proceeded with as the ground is cleared. The autumn seed-beds of cabbages should be sown in the second week of this month—if sooner the plants run to seed, if later they will not grow strong plants. The shelled corn found after a day's harvesting in the bottoms of carts should be collected for future use. The parings from corn-stacks should be gathered together for the same purpose. Store pigs may be run on the stubbles as soon as the corn is harvested.

SEPTEMBER.

The winter season for pork commences with this month, and pigs which were born in the early part of the year find a trade. There is food for the stores on the stubbles. Potato-digging is general, and a supply of food is generally available, as there are always diseased and injured potatoes to be disposed of. Drumhead cabbages are now fit for feeding, and provide food until Christmas. Nights get colder, and small pigs should be properly housed at night.

OCTOBER.

All young pigs should be kept warm, as the autumn rains and cold weather quickly produce chills. Older pigs may range on the stubbles, and after acorns, but should be supplied with extra food, and only allowed to be out for a short time. By the end of the month it is advisable to have all pigs in the yard. Winter sometimes sets in in October, and it is well to consider it a winter month, as by preparing for it loss is prevented. Mangels and potatoes should be got up before the end of the first week of November. Young sows should go to the boar.

NOVEMBER AND DECEMBER.

November is a good month to put the young sows or yilts to the boar. Those born in the early months of the year should go to the boar when they are eight or nine months old. Little pigs require very warm housing. It is better to buy strong stores than those directly from the sows at this season. Turnips, carrots, and cabbages are the best green food at this season. Potatoes (if cooked) are very valuable, and should never be wasted; they, however, must not be depended upon as a diet. These two are among the most difficult months for the pig keeper, because of the cold damp weather, and he cannot attend too closely to the warmth and comfort of the sties.

Begin the year, and continue to the end of the year, with the motto that cleanliness and warmth with regard to the sties form the first principle towards successful pig keeping. And never forget that the pig will turn to profitable account much that would otherwise be lost, and you will then find the truth of the old adage, " Waste not, want not."

INDEX.

Acorns, 67
Age—
    by Dentition, 32
    to Breed, 73
Ailments, 110
    Chills, 92
    Constipation, 115
    Coughs, 113
    Cramp, 92, 114
    Diarrhœa, 114
    Foot and Mouth Disease, 113
    Going off Feet, 83
    Inflammation of the Udder, 88
    Measles, 113
    Milk Fever, 81
    Rheumatism, 114
    Rupture, 87
    Scour, 92, 115
    Stybaked, 92
    Swine Fever. 110
    Trichinosis. 114
Allotments, 58, 105
April, 124
August, 126
Barley, 58
    Meal, 59
Beans, 63, 109
Bedfordshire, 10
Beech Mast, 67
Berkshire, 8
    Society, 19
Betony, 83, 113
Bleeding, 118
Boar—
    Selection, 35
    Management, 100
    Age to use, 101

Bran, 66
Breeds, 3
Breeds, Modern, 9
    Bedfordshire, 10
    Berkshire, 10, 18
    Black, Small, 10, 21
    Chester, White, 10
    Dorset, 10
    Essex, 10
    Poland-China, 9
    Suffolk, 10
    Tamworth, 10, 19
    White, 10
    Yorkshire, Large, 10, 11
        Middle, 10, 16
        Small, 10, 14
Breeding, 73
    Age, 73
    Season. 73
Breeds, Original—
    Berkshire. 8
    Cheshire. 8
    Chinese. 6
    English. 6
    Essex, 9
    Gloucestershire. 8
    Herefordshire. 8
    Liecestershire, 7
    Lincolnshire, 7
    Neapolitan, 6
    Norfolk, 8
    Northamptonshire, 8
    Rudgwick, 9
    Suffolk, 8
    Sussex, 9
    Wiltshire, 8
    Yorkshire, 7
Brown. Professor, 33

K

Buildings, adapting existing, 46
    Do. illustrated, 49
Building Sties, 40
    Construction, 44
    Drainage, 45
    Economy in, 40
    Exercise Courts, 43
    Features of Construction, 43
    Feeding Shutes, 43
    Flooring of the Sty, 50
    Front Elevation of Sties, 50
    Range of, 45
    Roofing, 41
    Shute, 45
    Size of, 46
    Slatted Floors, 51
    of Timber, 46
    Ventilation, 44
    Warmth, 40
Buttermilk, 70
Cabbages, 57, 68
Calendar, 122
Carrots, 68, 107
Castration, 86
Cheshire, 8
Chester White, 10
Chinese Pig, 6
Cinders, 71
Clover, 57, 108
Constipation, 115
Coal, 72
Cooking 54, 55
Corn Crops, 109
Corn Grinder or Grittler, 62
Cottager's Pig, 102
    Food for, 102, 104
    Sty for, 103
Cow Grass, 109, 113
Cramp, 114
Dairy Waste, 57
Dan, 66
December, 127
Dentition, 32
    Breaking Teeth, 80
Diarrhœa, 115
Domestic Pig, 5
Dorset, 10
Down-pigging Sows, 77
Epsom Salts, 85, 88
Essex, 9

Farm Offal, 57
Features of Trade, 119
February, 123
Feeding—
    Heavy Pigs, 97
    Young Pigs, 90
Feeding Stuffs (see Food), 54 57
    Shutes, 43
Food, 57
    Barley & Barley Meal, 58. 59
    Beans, 63
    Beech Mast, 67
    Bran, 63, 91
    Brewers' Grains, 70
    Buttermilk, 68
    Cabbages, 57, 68
    Carrots, 68
    Clover, 57, 69
    Coal and Cinders, 72
    Cooking, 54, 55
    Corn Grinder, 62
    Dairy Waste, 57, 70
    Dan, 66
    Farm Offal, 57
    Fermented, 57, 60
    Grass, 64
    Hogweed, 70
    Lentils, 65
    Lucerne, 69, 108
    Maize, 63
    Mangels, 57, 106
    Middlings, 66
    Oats, 63
    Parsnips, 68
    Peas, 65
    Pollard, 66
    Potato Cleaning, 54
    Potato Disease, 56
    Potatoes, 54, 58
    Purchasing, 61
    Rice, 65
    Roots, 68
    Sainfoin, 60
    Seconds, 66
    Stubbles, 69
    Turnips, 76, 107
    Vetches, 57
    Wash, 91
    Wheat, 63
    Whey, 68, 70

Foot and Mouth Disease, 113
Garden, 102
    Providing Food in, 105
    Waste, 69
Gestation, 74
Gloucestershire, 8
Grains, Brewers', 71
Grass, 57, 69
Herefordshire, 8
Hog Cholera, 110
Hogweed, 70
Housing (see Building Sties), 40
Influence—
    of District, 24
    of Popular Taste, 24, 27
January, 122
July, 125
June, 125
Lawes', Sir J. B., Experiments, 59, 64
Leguminous Crops, 69
Leicestershire, 7
Lice, 116
Lincolnshire, 7
Litter or Bedding, 52
Litters, Small, 37
Lucerne, 69, 108
Madder (see Betony), 83
Mange, 116
Management of Pigs, 90
Mangels, 57, 76, 106
Maize, 63
    and Grass in America, 64
Manure from Slatted Floors, 51
March, 123
May, 124
Mealmen, Honest and Dishonest, 61
Meal Worms, 61
Measles, 113
Medicating Pigs, 116
Middle White, 16
Middlings, 66
National Pig Breeders' Association, 12, 15, 21, 23
Neapolitan Breed, 6
Norfolk, 8
Northamptonshire, 8
November, 127
Oats, 63

October, 126
Parsnips, 68, 107
Parturition, 78
    Sow after, 81
Peas, 65, 109
Peccary, 3
Pedigree, 5
Pigs—
    in Health and Sickness, 82
    Medicating, 117
    Price of, 104
    Rate of Increase, 120
    Ringing, 117
    the Sucking, 82
Pig Calendar, 122
Pig Trade, Features of, 119
Points—
    of Essex, 8, 9
    of Large White, 13
    of Small White, 15
    Value of, 30
Poland-China, 9
Porker, 75
Potatoes, 54, 56, 58, 68
Purchase of Pigs, 38
    of Meal and Corn, 61
Rats, 112
Rearing, 91
Rheumatism, 92
Roots, 68
Rudgwick, 8
Ruptured Pigs, 87
Sainfoin, 69, 108
Scavenging, 57, 97
Score of 20 lbs., 26
Scour, 96
Seconds, 66
Selection—
    of Boar, 35
    of Sow, 36
    of Stock, 24
September, 126
Small Black, 10
Small Litters, 37
Sow—
    at Weaning, 89
    Down-pigging, 77
    Eating Young, 37
    Exercise for, 75
    In Pig, 75

Sow (*continued*)—
    Maiden, 39
    Number of Teats, 37
    Purchase, 38
    Size of Litter, 37
    Temper, 37
Spaying, 86
Stag, 101
Sties—
    Building, 40
    Fittings of, 52
    Steamer and Boiler, 55
    Troughs, 53, 54
Stock Selection, 24
    Vigorous, 28
Store Pigs, 26, 67
Stubbles, 69
Stybaked, 92
Sucking Pig, 85
Suffolk, 8, 10
Sussex, 8

Tamworth, 10
Taste, Popular, 24
Trade, Best Season, 73
Trough—
    Circular, 53
    Iron, 53
    with Double Sides, 54
Tuley, Joseph, 12
Turnip, 76, 107
Vermin, 116
Vetches, 57, 109
Wash, 91
Washtub, 70
Weaning, 87
    the Sow at, 89
Wheat, 63
Whey, 68, 70
Wild Hog, 3, 4
Worms, 116
Yilts, 39, 73
Yorkshire, 7

REDUCED FAC-SIMILE OF FRONT
OUTSIDE OF COVER.

Order regularly from any Railway Bookstall or Newsagent.   32 Pages, 3d.

EST 1796

BELL'S WEEKLY MESSENGER

PRICE THREE PENCE

JOHN BELL, ORIGINAL PROPRIETOR
THE TIMES OF AGRICULTURE

COUNTRY GENTLEMAN *&* LANDOWNERS' JOURNAL

No. 5029.   SATURDAY, JULY 13, 1895.   Price 3d.

CONTENTS

The Right Hon. W. H. Long, M.P.

Offices: 109, STRAND, LONDON, W.C.

Prepaid Subscriptions (Post free): 3 Months, 3s. 9d.; 6 Months, 7s. 6d.; 12 Months, 15s.

Mark Lane Express

THE
LEADING BRITISH AUTHORITY ON AGRICULTURE AND STOCK-BREEDING.

Offices: 150, STRAND, LONDON, W.C.

Published every MONDAY EVENING. Price 3d,

The "Mark Lane Express" contains articles on every branch of Agriculture and Stock-breeding by the highest authorities, the latest market intelligence, and are the pioneers of correct illustrations of Live Stock.

All interested in Agriculture or Live Stock should take the "Mark Lane Express" regularly by ordering from any Newsagent, Bookstall, or direct from the Office, post free, payable in advance, 1 year, 15s.; 6 months, 7s. 6d.

The "Mark Lane Express" is acknowledged by all classes of advertisers to be the very best medium for Agricultural Advertisements, and its columns are used by a greater number of them than any other agricultural paper.

All Orders for Advertisements should be sent to the Publisher.

Advertisements cannot be guaranteed insertion in proper position unless received by Saturday morning. No advertisement can be stopped or altered after Friday.

INCLUDING PORTRAIT PLATES OF NOTED LIVE STOCK &c.

Three Months ...	...	...	3s. 9d.
Six Months	...	...	7s. 6d
Twelve Months	...	...	15s. 0d.

United States and Canada, 4·50 dollars, Australia, Tasmania, New Zealand, &c., 17s. 6d. France and Belgium, 22 francs. Germany, 17½ marks per annum, post free.

All remittances for Subscriptions or Advertisements to be sent to the Publisher,
"MARK LANE EXPRESS," 150, Strand, London, W.C.
Cheques and Post Office Orders, crossed, London and Westminster Bank.

EDWIN BUSS,

ELPHICKS, HORSMONDEN, KENT,

BREEDER OF

Pedigree Large White Yorkshire and Berkshire Pigs.

HIGHEST AWARDS AT ROYAL SHOWS.

Breeder and Exhibitor in 1895 of the celebrated Berks Sow

" ELPHICKS MATCHLESS "

(SOLD TO AMERICA THE SAME SEASON FOR £45),

Winner of three Firsts and two Champions at three shows.

The Awards gained by the Yorkshire Pigs in 1895 at four leading shows were two Champions, five Firsts, two Seconds, and two Commendeds, with 14 entries.

All Communications receive prompt attention.

VISITORS ALWAYS WELCOME.

This Journal has a greater circulation by many thousands per week than any other Agricultural or similar paper in the United Kingdom.

Farm Field & Fireside

An Agricultural, Rural, and Domestic Journal.

FOR THE COUNTRY GENTLEMAN, FARMER, RURAL AND SUBURBAN RESIDENT,

AND ALL INTERESTED IN

The Farm, the Dairy, Live Stock, the Stable, Poultry, Garden, or the Home.

In all cases where possible, it is advisable to obtain the Paper through a Newsagent, Railway Bookstall, or Bookseller. If, however, it is not obtainable at the published price, it can be ordered direct from the Publishing Office, post free, at the following rates, payable in advance :—

ONE YEAR, 6s. 6d.   HALF-YEAR, 3s. 3d.

A Journal for Everybody.

QUERIES AND ANSWERS.

Especial attention is called to this feature of the paper, as the columns of every department of "FARM, FIELD, & FIRESIDE" are freely open to all, and offer a means of exchanging opinions and obtaining information such as can be met with in no other way.

N.B.—"FARM, FIELD, & FIRESIDE" offers a greater number of pages of well-printed useful information in a handy, compact form, Illustrated, stitched and cut, for the sum of

ONE PENNY.

Specimen Copies can be obtained from Newsagents, Booksellers, and Bookstalls, or direct from the Publishing Office,

1, Essex Street, Strand, London, W.C.

www.ingramcontent.com/pod-product-compliance
Lightning Source LLC
Chambersburg PA
CBHW021815190326
41518CB00007B/598